THE MAGICIAN OF THE SWATCHWAYS

A biography of

Maurice Griffiths

*MG's usual
cruising ground*

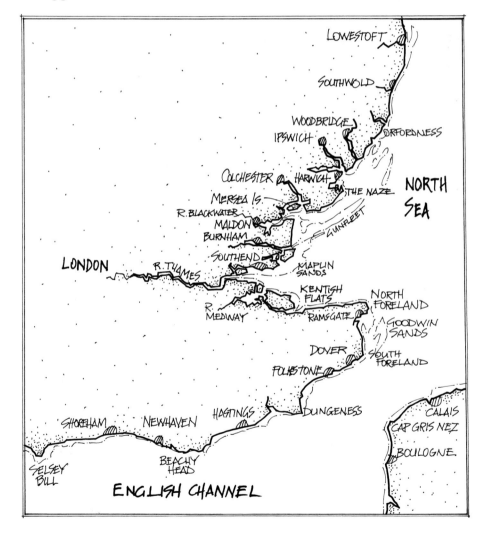

THE MAGICIAN
OF THE
SWATCHWAYS

A Biography of Maurice Griffiths

Dick Durham

"........and did it matter then a tinker's damn that it
was, after all, very small beer indeed?"
Maurice Griffiths, Ten Small Yachts

Dedication

For Cathy

By the same author

The Last Sailorman
On & Offshore: Cruising the Thames and the East Coast
Where the River Meets the Sea

Editor Geoff Pack
Design & Production Trevor Ridley

Published by
Yachting Monthly
IPC Magazines Ltd
King's Reach Tower
Stamford Street
London SE1 9LS

First Edition 1994
© Copyright IPC Magazines and Dick Durham 1994

ISBN 1 85277 096 1

Printed in Hong Kong by
Worldprint

Contents

Acknowledgements

My thanks go to all the friends and acquaintances of Maurice Griffiths who helped with their memories of the man.

They include: Dr. Paul Haigh, Des Sleightholme, Tony Purnell, Phil Sheaf, Norman Clackson, Jack Coote, John Williams, Cecil and Robert Barclay, Dennis Bird, Andrew Blyth, Frank Knights, Robert Simper, Ted Williams and Brian and Jennifer Brooke-Smith.

My thanks also go to Jimmy Green of St Mawes in Cornwall for his recollections of Peter Gerard and to Peter Willetts of Estuary Marine Services for his excellent library of Yachting Monthly backnumbers and to Nicholas Titshall for access to his collection of antiquarian yachting books

Preface

Maurice Griffiths' cabin rocks no longer on the ripples of an East Coast creek, but it is still cut off by the tide. His little bungalow, beneath some of the largest Scots pines on Mersea island, is severed from the mainland by a moat consisting of waters from the rivers Blackwater and Colne and the creeks of Pyefleet and Mersea Quarters. From the Coast Road Maurice still looks out towards the forbidding black oyster shed which stands on stilts embedded in the saltings of Packing Marsh Island. The muddy sides of this marshy islet act as his tide gauge. From the amount of glistening brown mud showing, Maurice knows whether or not the Strood causeway linking Mersea with the rest of Essex is under water. He senses relief when Packing Marsh Island tells him he is marooned, for then he is back aboard the craft of his youth, isolated from the beck and call of daily life ashore.

The cabin has been for Maurice both sanctuary and study through his long years; the cabin with its "all-pervading smell of damp bedding, wet sails, tarred rope, paraffin, dead stove

Nightfall's *cabin, illustrated by Maurice*

ashes, trapped air and rusty bilge water" transformed by the coal stove and the oil lamp into "the warmest and cosiest place imaginable. The essence of yachting".

His yacht *Nightfall* had perhaps the best cabin he ever lived in. Lined with mahogany and beechwood panelling, a skylight sent down dusty shafts of sunlight onto a varnished leaf table. There was a figured carpet on the cabin sole that matched the red cushions and backrests over which carved rails "like miniature banisters" ran the length of the shelves. Above, mahogany coachroof beams "arched darkly against the white deckhead". On the after bulkhead a filigreed brass oil lamp used a mirror to double its illumination - a soft, warm light.

Such cabins are not created any more and one wonders whether Maurice could have written 'The Magic of the Swatchways', the book, which when all else is forgotten about Maurice Griffiths, will alone serve him for posterity, in a modern yacht's cabin, so many of which appear to MG as "cold and stark as a hospital operating theatre".

When the moat has ebbed away and Mersea is reunited with Essex once more the great sands of the Buxey and the Gunfleet rise from the sea. Though they muzzle the approaches to the Blackwater and Colne they make Maurice feel secure. The peculiarity of the East Coaster is that, surrounded by sandbanks, he feels safe.

Maurice is a seaman who has navigated by improvisation and initiative. The course marks on his charts would not necessarily have avoided hazards; more often than not they would have bisected them.

Such a sailor is a delta man and one of the greatest deltas criss-crossed by sailors in the UK is that found on the East Coast between Lowestoft and the North Foreland. Maurice Griffiths is a delta man, a man at home in the Thames Estuary.

There are few sandbanks from the Nore to the Knock, the Gunfleet to the Girdler that the keels of his yachts haven't touched. Yet he has never lost a boat and has used the channels that run between them and the swatchways that run across them as his highways and byways for over 60 years.

The sands themselves act as moles and breakwaters for the true East Coaster:-

"Knowing some of these anchorages in the Thames Estuary where an expanse of drying sands can make a very useful harbour with the wind in the right direction... Although shoals to windward when the tide covers them are naturally not so effective as a firm weather shore, nevertheless even at high water they do calm down the seas to some extent and to leeward of them there is nothing like the turmoil that you would find on the windward side of the shoal."

That is the voice of the East Coaster - somebody at home sailing through a shallow maze - but he warns those novices who would follow him to sea of the "gimlet-eyed gentlemen" selling yachts at the Boat Show.

"A fin keel racing yacht with deep draught is not intended for sand navigation and cruising adventures... our type of boat must be able to take the ground, whether hard or soft, without damaging herself, and also without lying so far over as to risk filling on the next tide before she picks up and floats."

Now, however, Maurice has dropped "Old Cold Nose" for the last time. He is anchored in the hinterland of Mersea for good.

The fug of fried eggs and bacon laced with coal smoke is just a memory now. Yet as I sat in the cosy study of "MG's" home there was a hint of the old magic still. It wasn't the brass oil lamp gleaming from the wall. Nor the half models of his successful designs hanging next to watercolours of his favourite yachts. Nor yet was it the leather-bound copies of 'Yachting Monthly', the magazine he edited for 40 years, lining the companionway which led out to the hall of his bungalow at West Mersea. It was to be many visits before I realised what spell it was that charmed me, but gradually I came to understand my bewitching. I noticed how often Maurice sat listening to my questions with his long, delicate fingers steepled under his chin. I noticed too how the cover was always off his typewriter and that invariably a sheet of paper was rolled in the carriage ready to take the patter of keys. It was the most significant object in that little room - his old-fashioned, sit-up-and-beg style typewriter.

So I learned how Maurice himself sat up and via a succession of old portables begged a living with articles and literally wrote himself out of poverty. Also how since then he has never been without a trusty typewriter - neither ashore nor afloat.

It was as a teenager at home in Gippeswyk Avenue, Ipswich, that Maurice tentatively sent out articles about the local Orwell yacht races to the 'East Anglian Daily Times' to begin his writing career. A few publications encouraged him further - and Maurice was never a man who needed much encouragement - to write a little book on his experiences running a yacht agency. It was called 'Yachting on a Small Income'.

The year before this first book was published, 1925, his father Walter died suddenly and unexpectedly.

Maurice was 22 years old when along with his mother, Lena, he was thrown out onto the streets. Walter had run up massive debts through gambling and womanizing. The home, the furniture and Maurice's current boat, *Storm*, as well as the fledgling yacht agency he had begun all had to be sold to pay off the bank.

His mother went to live with her sister in Lincolnshire. His brother, Leslie, was married with a son and lived in the far away Midlands.

Maurice quickly weighed up the situation. Should he try to get a job on the local press or chance his arm in London on the nationals? He decided on the Dick Whittington route and soon regretted it.

Cooped up in damp bedsits around Euston he batted away at his typewriter. By night a sputtering gas ring gave him warmth as he wrote, while by day he bravely touted his meticulously laid out typescripts around busy and indifferent editorial offices.

There were some successes - short stories for the 'Evening Standard' and the now defunct 'Evening News', even cookery items for 'Vogue' magazine half remembered from amateur flour and water recipes dreamed up aboard *Storm*.

There was also acre after acre of copy about boats. They liked his words at a magazine called the 'Yacht Owner'. They started publishing much of his work, but the cheques never arrived. In their offices on the Strand a gaunt-faced Maurice was told not to worry; he would get all he was owed after the next issue came out. This continued until one day there was no next issue. The magazine folded owing Maurice a desperately needed small fortune.

In that same Strand reception room he met another journalist who was also now penniless - Dulcie Kennard. She wrote under the byline 'Peter Gerard' and they were later to marry.

Maurice was semi-starving when another magazine, 'Fore An' Aft', published in America, started taking both his and Peter's copy. There were articles on anything from cementing the bilges of ancient boats to the benefits of sailing Dutch botters. Try as he might though, Maurice could not break into the rarefied atmosphere that then pervaded 'Yachting Monthly'. They wanted social stories surrounding the elite yachting brigade who frequented Cowes and other prestigious venues. Items about concreted garboard strakes were dismissed at a glance.

One of the frustrations I faced over the hours spent with a tape-recorder grilling Maurice about his long life was trying to pin him down on absolutes. However, later as I flicked through back numbers of these yellowing magazines, I came to the conclusion it was an old habit that had kept him in bread and butter. Shrewdly Maurice realised that definitive comment meant finite copy. If he condemned gaff against bermudian, hard chine against round bilge, clinker against carvel he would soon have antifouled himself out of the boat-yard.

In the end it was Maurice's first book that provided his deliverance. Picked up at a railway station bookstall by the manager of 'Yachting Monthly', George Bittles, it immediately struck a chord. George wanted to start a sister paper to YM called 'Yacht Sales And Charters' and, having read Maurice's book, he asked him to edit it.

Now Maurice was installed in a warm office, with a regular wage, but 'Yacht Sales and Charters' didn't last long - the big yacht agencies baulked at such competition and started withdrawing their advertising from 'Yachting Monthly' itself. However, Maurice was up and running now and within a year he was editor of YM where he gave a helping hand to Peter Gerard and took her copy. This was no great sacrifice however as she wrote very well.

Although he is best known for 'The Magic of the Swatchways', his most successful book, Maurice in fact wrote an obsessional 19 books.

Those months of near despair were a lesson he was never to forget. No fewer than 15 books were published on yachting and yacht designing, some of them going into Dutch and Polish editions. If we include 'Yachting on a Small Income' and 'Magic' the list is as follows:

      'Ten Small Yachts and Others'
      'Little Ships and Shoal Waters'
      'Cruising Yarns From The YM'
      'Post-War Yachting'
      'Dream Ships'
      'Everyman's Yachting'
      'Sailing on a Small Income'
      'Arrow Book of Sailing'
      'Swatchways and Little Ships'
      'Man the Shipbuilder'

'The First of the Tide'
'Round the Cabin Table'
'Sixty Years a Yacht Designer'

There were also three novels - 'The Sands of Sylt', inspired by Erskine Childers classic 'Riddle of the Sands'; 'Dempster and Son', a story of railway folk sparked off from Maurice's first love, namely the steam trains he, as a boy, watched shunt into Ipswich station from Gippeswyk Avenue where the Victorian houses backed on to the sidings and turntable; and 'No Southern Gentleman', an American Civil War romance.

'The Hidden Menace', which was published in 1981, is a tome on the history of mine warfare gleaned from his days in the RNVR helping to defuse German parachute bombs, a task for which he received the George Medal. Maurice did not need to keep on writing. He had taken over at YM in 1927 and, as well as the pressures of editing an increasingly popular magazine, was, within a year, also earning money from designing yachts. His first cruising yacht, *Wind Song*, being built in 1928. Even Maurice himself admitted to me that he thought he'd over cooked it. As I took various editions of his books to him to sign, on behalf of family and friends, he stopped once and said, "This makes me feel 'My God have I produced all these?' I was a bit of a workaholic. I think I probably overdid it."

It was a case of once hungry twice victualled.

Like those who can remember what they were doing when J F Kennedy was assassinated, I can recall where I was when first I came under that peculiar spell of Maurice's lyricism. It was in Aldeburgh in 1965 while thumbing through 'Magic of the Swatchways' in the mildewed yacht club library. I had sailed there on my father's Belouga, *Mouette*. He had gone off to pick my mother and sister up from the railway station so that we could all be together for a family holiday. While he was gone I slumped in a damp armchair and read about the voice of the shingle, the silent creeks.

Here is Maurice sitting in the cockpit of his little barge-yacht, *Swan*, anchored in Beaumont Creek in the Walton Backwaters as his dinner is cooking:

"It was eerie and lonely out here, and somehow every sound ceased, as though the rest of the world had suddenly been cut off, and I instinctively pulled the collar of my jacket up and slipped my hands under the lapels. A dead, uncanny silence reigned over everything. And now the mist was around us, blotting out everything but the dark mass of the dinghy as it rested on the mud and the four yellow beams of light that escaped through the portlights.

"An owl hooted with startling suddenness from a far-off spinney. The queer raucous voice rose to a hideous shriek like a soul in agony, and seemed to rend the fog with its outlandish cacophonous horror. A screech-owl, unholy prophet of untold miseries... But I became aware of a slight odour that brought me violently to my senses again, causing me to leave my hard seat precipitately and dash into the warm cabin. That stew had just begun to 'catch'."

By the time my father returned he had an incurable romantic for a crew.

Father, mother and sister took bed and breakfast in a local pub. I slept on board listening to the tide and dreaming of dangerous bars and friendly withies.

Maurice Griffiths could enslave a schoolboy with a few paragraphs about supper in a half-tide creek. Basil Lubbock had clippers foundering off Cape Horn and, in my opinion, was still boring.

Maurice's prose has provided real comfort to many of his readers. The following came in a letter to me from one of his disciples as far away as New Zealand:

"I have long lost count of the number of times I have read them all (his books) and I have always turned to them in times of stress, or depression, particularly business worries, as the best means of relaxation and composure. I think it is their aura of peace of mind and tranquillity, that emanates from Maurice's descriptions that has the desired effect."

So when 26 years later I came to write Maurice Griffiths' biography it was a slightly surreal experience to meet the man I felt I'd already known as a 14 year-old.

A light sou'westerly breeze was cracking the Terylene sails of dinghies about to be wheeled into the glittering summer tide as I drove to his new home, deliberately built up and away from the coast. He has not exactly turned his back on the waters from which he wrought a great career, for twice a month he will drive down to West Mersea Yacht Club with his second wife, Coppie, for lunch. There they will take a table with a view over the Quarters and watch. But it has inevitably changed. Maurice has not been afloat for many years now and he has not owned a boat since he broke his leg aboard his last yacht, *Kylix*. It was with no great regret, however, that he left the creeks he had enjoyed so much.

As he observed after a display from some waterskiers on one of his last cruises to Hamford Water, in the Walton

Backwaters, probably his best loved spot: "In comparison with noise-making sports like motorcycle racing, football, speedboating, or even private flying, it is not necessarily a holier-than-thou attitude to think of small boat sailing and cruising as a form of pleasure that need cause no inconvenience to others.

"With your little home about you, and the warm lamplight in the cabin inviting you below when the evening air begins to feel chilly, you have with you everything a man or woman may need to feel at peace with a world which at such times can seem far, far away."

By the time I came to meet the man himself his "little home" was permanently moored on dry land.

I secured the job of writing MG's biography after he generously reviewed my own sailing book, 'On and Offshore: Cruising the Thames and the East Coast'. He had passed the book on to a friend of his, Phil Sheaf, with whom I corresponded and to whom I wondered idly whether anyone had considered writing MG's life story. The next I knew MG himself wrote to say that as far as he was aware no one was in fact doing a book and he would assist me with as much research as he could.

The door of his bungalow was open letting in the warm summer air when first I visited him in July 1991. A frail, spare man with a white, grizzled beard hiding the lantern jaw line of a still handsome face greeted me with shy, exquisite manners.

In his little shore based cabin over the course of several months I began asking the first questions about a life nearly 90 years old.

At last when I felt I had exhausted my researches into the subject I called one day and told Maurice I had started writing, that as a result I felt a sense of relief. The articulate fingers steepled. The steady blue eyes fixed mine with a concentration built of long discipline. I wriggled. Out of habit Maurice moved his chair a little nearer his typewriter.

"Yes," he said. "Starting a book is rather like priming a pump."

1

An Ipswich Childhood

Anyone listening to the incongruously aristocratic diction of Maurice Griffiths would find it hard to believe he was born a Cockney. Yet dressed in a smart reefer jacket and with the tie of the West Mersea Yacht Club knotted around his neck he was, in his ninetieth year, insistent that on 22nd May, 1902, Herne Hill in South London was still a manor from which you could hear Bow Bells.

During the early 1890s his father, Walter, the youngest of three brothers and one sister, children of Dr John Griffiths, had left the family surgery in Wolverhampton and moved to the capital in order to work in a glove warehouse owned by a company called Dent Allcroft.

His boss soon realised that Walter's impressive waxed moustache, his ruddy complexion, boisterous manner and booming voice would be best employed selling the product out on the road. Consequently in January 1903 he was promoted to salesman, covering East Anglia, and quickly had to find a suitable home within his patch.

Walter, then 32, considered moving his family to Norwich, but eventually settled on Ipswich. Maurice, swaddled in blankets, was slung round the bosom of his mother Selina, known as Lena in her family, and with his elder brother Leslie, left London by train from Liverpool Street.

For three years the family lived in a detached Victorian villa on the Woodbridge Road, but Walter found the distance to and from Ipswich station too great for his early morning and late night trains. So in 1906 the family moved again, this time to 10 Gippeswyk Avenue, a newly built row of red brick semis which overlooked the station. The road was lined each side with shady elms and led to the Elizabethan Gippeswyk Hall with its farm and woods beyond. It was entrancing country for a small boy, but in addition, across a narrow park, the house overlooked the Great Eastern main line where it left the station for the East Coast.

Leslie Griffiths (aged 14) and brother Maurice (7½)

Four year old Maurice would spend hours staring across the road at the great steam engines that puffed by beneath a row of elm trees. There was also a sorting yard just a quarter of a mile away.

At first Walter thought he had made a mistake - that the continual noise of the engines would drive them out, but soon the family got so used to the trains running to the Great Eastern timetable that they set their clocks by them.

Maurice's first love - which lasted throughout his life - was for those Prussian blue engines with their red coupling rods, polished brasswork and varnished teakwood coaches. He never complained when his father ordered him to brush his black silk top hat in the mornings for the job came before a walk to the station.

While Maurice cleaned his hat Walter would brush down his frock coat and striped trousers and settle his gold watch chain across his prominent paunch and into the pocket of his fawn waistcoat.

"He regarded himself as something of an elite in the glove-selling world," recalled Maurice with a reflective chuckle.

As his father travelled the flatlands of East Anglia on the Great Eastern system, convincing ladies they had cold hands, young Maurice built his own train network - a Gauge 1 model railway - in the attic room he had been allotted for his now all consuming passion.

He was helped by a school friend, Claude Leathers, and another lad held in awe by Maurice and Claude as his father actually worked on the railway. Together the boys made their own steel track, pointwork, stations, bridges, signal boxes, wooden trucks and coaches. The clockwork and steam locos kept them up in the loft for hours.

Their scaled down knowledge of railways helped them understand the real thing and the lads knew where to put half-pennies on the line so they would not jump off. The resulting pancaked coin they tried to exchange for a penny's worth of sweets. Unfortunately the confectioner concerned was not convinced by the clumsy counterfeit.

Another large railway sorting yard, where the boys flattened their coins, was near Ipswich Docks. In those days spritsail shadows danced over the rail tracks leading to the dockside. Sailing barges could regularly be seen discharging there as well as the occasional square rigger.

Maurice's first lasting maritime impression, however, was of a steamship, which was the largest ship ever to squeeze through the lock at Ipswich. This was thought novel enough to throw the craft open to the public and Lena took Maurice aboard. "I remember being struck by the open fire blazing away in the cabin," he said. It seemed that ships could be like homes.

Soon Mr and Mrs Griffiths took Maurice for river trips down the Orwell to Harwich and Felixstowe aboard the Great Eastern Railway's paddle steamers - *Norfolk*, *Essex* and *Suffolk*. As they passed Butterman's Bay the young Maurice

Barges at the Spitway
M. Griffiths

*The old
Margate Hook
Beacon*
M. Griffiths

gazed at the tall masts of square rigged ships, among them *Lawhill* and others, discharging into barges.

Maurice's mother wanted a good start for her youngest son. Her eldest, Leslie, had emigrated to Canada. He had never got on well with his father and had moved away as soon as he could. Lena, therefore, wanted Maurice, who, though seven years younger than Leslie, already seemed brighter, to do something with his life. She put him down for Queen Elizabeth's Grammar School in Henley Road as a day boy, but when Walter found out he was furious - he did not want to pay the fees. Instead he intended to send Maurice to the cheaper Municipal School. Lena, however, won the day and Maurice's manners, if not his mind, were the better for it.

Lena was a volatile woman originally from Hereford. She had passionate periods of intense interest in various subjects - from philosophy to theosophy - her "crazes" as Walter dismissed them. She ignored his disinterest and went on by 1912 to become a confirmed suffragette, taking Maurice to rowdy meetings in the town where he was impressed by his mother's excitement at the cry "Votes for Women".

Walter raged against his wife's insubordination as he saw it, citing the more extreme actions of the suffragettes, such as torching postboxes and chaining themselves to railings, as being evidence of their unsuitability to be part of the electorate.

"His face took on a heated appearance if the word suffragette was mentioned," said Maurice.

Maurice preferred it when Lena took him to St Lawrence Church, in the town, where she was the organist. He had the demanding job of working the organ handle fast enough to keep up with his mother's enthusiasm.

Leslie returned from Canada when war broke out in 1914. He became an infantryman in the 6th Suffolk Regiment and was gassed on the Somme. He survived the war, but never fully recovered from the mustard gas. He married a girl called Lil; the couple had a daughter, Molly, and moved in over Lena's sister's ironmongery store in Spalding, Lincolnshire.

Soon after the First World War started, young Maurice noticed with dismay how the Great Eastern trains no longer gleamed with blue paint or polish. They were now painted black or grey and delays were so frequent, because of troop trains, that the service was redundant as a free clock.

His father - who always used the train as he had a fear of motorcars - became as drab as the coaches, which were now shabby and flea-ridden, that he travelled on. Out went the top hats, the flowered buttonholes. Instead he wore a felt hat, jacket and trench coat. No longer did he simply carry samples of ladies' gloves. Walter was now expected to cart round general haberdashery for men and women.

"Dad was a very old-fashioned gentleman and now he had to take all these beastly samples - women's underwear as well as gloves," said Maurice.

The station hotels he had used so often lost their luxury and

Barges taking freight in Butterman's Bay
M Griffiths

glamour as the heating was turned off and the menu choice cut back.

The fine suede gloves - one of which stretched the length of a lady's arm holding a globe for the company motto "Hand-in-glove with the World" - were now in "short supply". Leather was used for the harnesses of horse drawn field guns in the mud of Flanders, and officers' belts and leggings took miles of hide as well.

As the first Zeppelin raids bombed East Anglia, Walter, too old now for the Forces, was issued with a revolver, truncheon and armband marked "SC" as he joined the Special Constables to patrol the streets of Ipswich. For her part Lena served with the St John Ambulance.

Walter's working war years were spartan ones. He longed for the good old days before the war when he spent too much money on whisky, champagne and cigars. Before his portly physique shrank through the frugalities of wartime existence, Walter enjoyed the company of women, indulging in a string of affairs.

"Although Mum and Dad had been passionately in love, Walter had a roving eye on his train travels. He was attractive to women, who proved expensive to keep up," says Maurice. "Life at number 10 was punctuated with stormy periods."

Walter was now almost constantly in debt, for he was a chronic gambler, betting regularly on horses and making risky investments.

Maurice left school as the war ended in 1918. He had made "little mark" in games or the classroom, except for history and English, for which he won prizes.

He got a job with Cornells, the auctioneers and estate agents in Princes Street. His mother persuaded him to stay on at home as support for her against the rages and at times violent behaviour of Walter.

"This often resulted in what was undoubtedly an over-mothering influence on me," says Maurice.

2

The First Boat

It was nearly five o'clock when two youths skidded their bicycles to a halt in the summer dust alongside Stalham staithe in one of the northernmost parts of the Norfolk Broads. They had peddled furiously from Stalham station, where the train had dropped them, to get to the boatyard before it closed.

The boat hirer was not sure about Claude Leathers' claim to be an experienced, seagoing yachtsman, but he was just an employee and it was time to go home. Thus Maurice and Claude hired the 24ft clinker-built sloop *Reindeer*, then made a fuss about getting their gear aboard, thus they ensured that the yardhand went home before they cast off and attempted to beat down Barton Broad in what was to be the first sail of their lives.

The amount of mud on *Reindeer*'s stem was evidence of their poor success in turning to windward and it was while they were stuck in the rushes that Maurice became fascinated by sails of another kind; those turning majestically on a windmill. He had a passing desire to grab one of the sails which seemed far less puzzling than *Reindeer*'s mainsail.

"I thought it would be so easy just to grab it," he said, but Claude talked him out of it. "It was just as well as I hadn't realised that I would have had to turn upside down at the top."

There were more thrills when the pair sailed the boat beneath a bridge, holding their breath as they went with pounding hearts in case it was too low, only to realise later that the mast was stepped in a lowering tabernacle for the very purpose of negotiating bridges.

In fact Maurice's first time under canvas came about mainly because of his love of trains. Their long rail journey up from Ipswich had been the holiday he had looked forward to, but Claude had older brothers who owned a 30ft smack yacht, *Gem*, and after crewing for them Claude wanted to go sailing as captain. However, after that first week's sailing on

Stalham and Barton Broads Maurice had the bug. All talk on the train home was of when he could get afloat again. Could he go sailing aboard *Gem* he wondered?

This was soon arranged and, said Maurice after a jaunt down the Orwell, "I thought 'By Jove' this is the thing. We decided we must have a boat of our own."

Outside the lock gates of Ipswich dock were about 30 yachts moored in The Bight. One, *Scoter,* took Maurice's eye and he looked lovingly at her, unwittingly absorbing every detail of her lines.

"I used to cycle down to the docks trying to keep my wheels from the sunken railway tracks and I remember falling in love with one yacht called the *Scoter*. She was a very beamy boat rather like a bawley, had a pole mast and long separate topmast. I thought 'That's the boat'. I didn't realise she was 15 tons. She had lovely deadeyes and lanyards and almost knee high bulwarks." Sadly, she was not for sale.

The one that was for sale was a 6 ton smack yacht, the 30ft *Undine*. Her straight stem and pretty, square counter gave her an aesthetic glow, which blinded the two young men to the concrete filling her 5ft 3in draught, which her owner said kept her stiff enough to win races, and to the fact that she had more copper tingles on her bottom than the gipsy flower sellers of Ipswich's Butter Market had patches on their shawls.

Maurice and Claude sold their Gauge 1 railway for £70, which was exactly the price of *Undine*. The old cutter, built in 1873, had been on the market for over a year at £100. The owner had recently reduced the price and could not believe his luck when the two "faces" turned up.

Maurice was by now writing articles on railways for the 'East Anglian Daily Times' and he began offering pieces on local yacht club events as well.

In that spring of 1921 he would not even consider a small dayboat as being suitable for a novice. The boat he would own must have a cabin, must have a blazing fire. Must be like a home.

"Our ignorance was abysmal. Undine had rot under the concrete and she wasn't easy to sail. She also had a draught too deep for sailing in our waters, but the strange thing was that most British yachts were built that way then. She was nothing unusual in that respect," says Maurice.

In their huge yacht the jolly sailors cast off from their moorings in The Bight. They were disappointed at her performance - she seemed very sluggish in stays. A mocking voice from a moored yacht they passed enquired whether they always set their jib upside down.

Then Maurice struck his first mudbank at Pond Ooze, "a nasty corner" between Ipswich and Pin Mill. It was to be the first impact in a long line of seabed sounding with *Undine*.

The tide was flooding and eventually *Undine* rose with the river and was steered seawards once more.

Further down river though, "Something seemed to have gone wrong with the tiller; it felt as though it had died in my hand. There was no longer any pressure on it as I held it close to the lee coaming and when I glanced over the lee rail the froth in the water was stationary, too."

The old gaff cutter slowly lay over, the tide ebbed away and her crew sat listening to the water trickling out of a poorly fitted tingle.

"That wretched deep keel and her sharp bottom gave me the urge to buy yachts that sat up decently when they were aground.

"It was from the experience of *Undine* that I began to wonder why yachts were built with deep, sharp bottoms. Why couldn't they be more like Thames barges? In those days there were many hundreds of Thames spritsail barges, commercial vessels. They sailed all round the coasts, put up with very bad weather, yet they were completely flat bottomed. So I got this slight complex... mania, you might call it, of wanting to have a yacht with an almost flat bottom, not such a deep keel."

With the exception of *Wilful* - in which Maurice cruised down Channel - he never bought a boat drawing over five feet again.

Undine was soon back on the market.

"I couldn't afford to keep a boat throughout the year, one year to another, so I would sail them in the summer and sell them in the autumn, then start again. It was quite easy to sell a boat then," says Maurice.

In this way he saved on laying up costs.

A yachtsman from the Walton & Frinton Yacht Club arrived with his paid hand to look over *Undine*.

"He was Commodore of the club and dressed like a Commodore, too. He was so taken with *Undine* that he paid £100 and took her away, even though the paid hand did not like her at all. A week or so later he took her out on the hard, realised what she was like and he was very cross indeed."

So cross was he indeed that when a more experienced Maurice came to write about *Undine* he changed her name to

Iduna. "She was in an awful state - cement almost up to the floorboards. I felt I had better not rub it in," Maurice explains.

Falling trade in house buying in the early twenties cost Maurice his job. After two years he was still the last to join Cornells' staff and was therefore first out. Undaunted he started his own agency - a yacht agency - based in the old attic where his railway had been.

Simply called 'Maurice Griffiths, Yacht Agent', the business prospered as the young Maurice bought and sold boats from 17ft to 36ft, learning more about craft as he traded. There were some illustrious names among his customers as well. In 1923 Chas Pears, ROI, the yachtsman, artist and author bought the boat he sailed for the rest of his life. She was *Wanderer*, a 10 ton Payne yawl built in 1881.

"He was a jolly fine man. A good old bluff Yorkshireman," says Maurice. "He gave me a good price for that yacht in those days - £425. It was a substantial figure because you could buy a fairly old but reasonable boat for £100 then."

Frank G G Carr, who became director of the National Maritime Museum at Greenwich, bought a 5 ton gaff cutter, *Lily*, built at Southend in 1904, which he renamed *Quickstep II* and unfortunately lost in the North Sea on his first offshore cruise.

Undine,
6 tons (built
1873)

3

Lone Sailor

Many scars had been carved in the mud of the Orwell from Bloody Point to Wherstead Ooze by *Undine*'s keel as her crew tried manfully to get her to sea, but they never felt a North Sea wave in the big yacht. *Undine*'s season under Claude and Maurice was restricted to the river and its banks.

It was in a far less suitable craft that Maurice made his first coastal passage.

Still smarting from the humiliations of *Undine*'s prohibitive keel, Maurice spent the autumn and early winter of 1921 searching the creeks of Essex and Suffolk on his bicycle for the right boat.

Eventually he found *Dabchick*, a 17ft converted ship's lifeboat with a bolted on lead keel giving her a draught of 3ft. The transom-sterned *Dabchick* had been used as a hire craft on the Broads; news that brought back happy memories for Maurice as he looked her over in her berth at Woodbridge. She had a lifting cabin top with collapsible canvas sides, rather like a fire bellows. Her compass binnacle was lit for night sailing with a candle.

Just after Christmas, Maurice, having paid £36 from the sale of *Undine* for *Dabchick*, went to deliver her to his mooring in the Bight.

"A blustery north wind was blowing little scurries of snow round the corners of the deserted streets and moaning through the telegraph wires above the local post office with a mournful wail that rose, every now and then, to an unearthly shriek. The electric arc light that was suspended over the centre of the square where the main thoroughfare crossed the station road was swinging about in the wind, casting its cold rays up and down the fronts of the houses as it rocked, while the sign over the door of the 'Boar's Head' squealed harshly as it swung to and fro.

"Two figures were making their way in the shadows down the narrow street leading to the footbridge over the railway,

Maurice's second boat, Vahan*: 17´x 6´x 3´ 1922. An old ship's boat converted to two berth gunter sloop*

and as they passed, a couple of locals paused before turning into the taproom of the 'Boar's Head' and stared after them.

"To explain why two somewhat determined-looking young men should be leaving behind them the cheerful lights of the little country town on this wild night and resolutely be making their way towards the pitchy darkness of the river, clad in old clothes and encumbered with two suitcases, a coil of rope, a hurricane lamp, some brown paper parcels that cried for tender support, and a fry-pan, briefly clothed in a negligee of local news, needs but three words.

"They were 'yachting'."

Thus Maurice sets the scene in the opening passage of 'The Magic of the Swatchways'.

He was now the proud owner of a poorly ballasted, narrow gutted, over tender hull with questionable fastenings, a huge lugsail rig designed for the benign catspaws and safety of the Norfolk Broads and that feature beloved by Maurice and which so often caused him to view the rest of a vessel through rose coloured spectacles - a cabin. It had blue linoleum on the cabin sole, was lined with pitchpine, and had two "plush-cushioned" berths; even Maurice conceded it was like a "kennel".

Maurice and his crew tossed a coin to decide which of them would have to strip off to retrieve the dinghy anchor now covered in freezing river water. Maurice lost, but the stalwarts were soon aboard with the cabin lamp and Primus stove building a fug in the little cabin.

Outside a wicked winter westerly hit the tree lined banks in mortar-like squalls. Fields of snow reflected an ominously clear moon, but in the cell-like cabin "...as we lay in our berths under warm blankets, sleep withheld her spell for a time while we listened to all the unaccustomed noises, trying to diagnose each one. The sudden rasp of the anchor chain on the bobstay, the tap tap of a halliard on the mast, the occasional squeak of a block in its eyebolt, the scrunch of the water against the lands of the planks, and over all the continuous roar of the wind in the trees that sheltered this snug anchorage."

Already Maurice was beginning to feel that heightened sense of well-being, of cosiness, of security that can only be felt when precariously close to that which threatens it. A house is a castle against the elements and therefore they are rarely noticed. On the other hand a tent is too flimsy ever to feel truly safe. It is a feeling peculiar only to the occupiers of small boat cabins.

The wind had not eased the following morning as the crew of *Dabchick* had hoped. Neither of them mentioned this though, and the little boat sped down past Felixstowe Ferry and headed for the treacherous shingle entrance with a six knot ebb for company.

That day the duty Coastguard could not believe his eyes. Here on this wild winter's morning was a large dinghy with a cabin built on it heading for the open sea. He left his warm quarters and ran down the shingle beach as *Dabchick* passed, to get the name and destination of a boat which, like as not, might prove to be the subject of anxious enquiries later in the day.

Dabchick burst her foresail in the first sea, and hit the bar. Maurice's crew, helming at the time, stripped off, plunged over the side and using his shoulder gave her a shove, clambering back aboard as she sailed clear.

They had been lucky and knew it. Yet once their passage was over and they were safely moored in The Bight, as they supped cups of Bovril and the Primus dried out the cabin, the young Maurice and his pal rationalized the dramas as proof of just how seaworthy the boat was.

That summer of 1922 was a windy one and Maurice battled with mainsheet and reef points, for the most part alone aboard *Dabchick*, which he renamed *Vahan*, a Sanskrit word meaning "vehicle for travel, or flights of fancy". There were too many *Dabchicks* on the coast for Maurice to feel unique in his new ship.

This was the first boat Maurice owned alone, but as he set off each weekend from his mooring in the Bight, he did not forget the lessons learned in his partnership with Claude Leathers. There were those vast muddy sides of the River Orwell for a start and *Vahan* made ridiculously short boards, well within the safety of the river proper, although she was two feet shallower than *Undine*, as Maurice nervously beat down to Harwich.

There was a great sense of achievement as the little boat remained mobile and opened out the waters of the River Stour. Yet there was more mud to come and it could threaten the very safety of the ship never mind just temporarily hinder her progress. On his first cruise alone Maurice found out just how vulnerable the little world of the floating home could become.

Here he is one night anchored above Parkston on the River Stour. "Below, the little cabin was warm and snug with the Primus heating up a stew and coffee and the wall lamp giving a soft glow to the varnished pitch-pine. The bows were scrunching into the little wind-blown waves that trickled noisily along the lands of the planks - a pleasant sound that is absent in carvel built boats - while I could hear the *splash splash* of the pram dinghy astern above the roar of the wind.

"Once during the night I woke up and looked out to find the rain gone and the stars overhead. A few lights still shone at Parkston, their reflections writhing across the troubled water like frantic snakes. For a long time I sat in the well, drinking in the wonder of a first night afloat, alone aboard my own little craft, independent of the land, cut off from civilisation, with the freedom of the sea awaiting me on the morrow. Only the cold night air drove me back to the warm blankets in the dark cabin."

Yet on "the morrow" while anchored off the Stone Heaps at the bottom end of the River Orwell he found himself on a lee shore in a northeast gale.

"I was violently awakened by rolling out of my bunk on to the cabin floor. *Vahan* seemed to have gone mad. She was twisting and turning and plunging viciously, rasping at her anchor chain under the keel as though caught in a maelstrom. The cabin clock by the light of the torch showed the time as a quarter past two."

Already we have the feel of the cosy world rudely interrupted by fate for there is no time to light the oil-lamp and read the clock by its reassuring amber glow. Action is required and time is fixed with the functional light of a torch, an illumination used in emergency.

Maurice had to get *Vahan* a tackable distance from the lee shore, so he hauled in the kedge anchor preparatory to rowing it out further to windward. As he dropped it aboard he noticed to his horror that he had picked up the main anchor as well.

"Almost immediately Vahan was ashore, lying over on her beam ends, while 4ft seas broke over her weather bilge and ran over her coamings into the well. For a time, in despair, I balanced on the weather rail, thinking that this was the end of my poor little ship. As she rose and fell the jarring was sickening, while below I could hear the crash of breaking crockery as the cups jumped off their hooks."

Now the cosy world is violated by the elements as domestic order is turned to chaos.

It is this juxtaposition of snare and sanctuary, danger and deliverance, running through Maurice's maritime adventures that makes them so appealing and the cabin is the leitmotif of his writings.

It is the cabin that enables the yachtsman to go away for the night, the cabin that distinguishes him as a cruising man; the cabin that enables him to make a passage and therefore to navigate, however fundamentally.

Maurice loved to make a passage at night ever since the time he did so aboard *Vahan* when the wind died on him off Clacton and he had to await a breeze in the early hours of the morning to get him into port.

"It seemed so wonderful to do that and afterwards I never had any fears in going round the coast in the dark. In fact I used to thoroughly enjoy a night sail. I suppose that's the germination of the whole idea of the magic," Maurice told me.

It had indeed been a magical passage. Maurice had witnessed the fairy green glow of phosphorescence for the first time and had successfully navigated his way, using Messum's 1903 edition of 'East Coast Rivers', into the Blackwater and up to the Nass beacon.

Next morning, as he found himself in a new world, he blinked in the sunlight at the square tower of West Mersea church, at the oyster smacks drifting in and out of the creeks he had negotiated the night before and he concluded:

"... when I saw this, was I not thrilled by the fun, the inward satisfaction of my first night of discovery, and did it matter then a tinker's damn that it was, after all, very small beer indeed?"

Maurice rowed ashore with a stone jar to fill with water. Here he met an old man sitting on the bench in the Coast Road. They exchanged pleasantries and the old chap extended his hand.

"I noticed he was wearing black gloves and it was very queer as there only appeared to be two fingers of the hand he offered me."

Maurice discovered the old gentleman was the father of one Fid Harnack, a name which would later grace the pages of 'Yachting Monthly' with his evocative paintings. Fid's father had been one of the pioneers of the X-ray and as such had not known about the effects of radiation.

The east coast of England runs from the mouth of the Tweed to the South Foreland, yet the East Coast of England, stretching from Orfordness to the North Foreland, is essentially the Thames Estuary and has capital letters thanks partly to the fact that Maurice Griffiths sailed in the area.

Sailing in this delta of what was, in Maurice's early days,

DABCHICK
always towed a
pram dinghy
M. Griffiths

the entrance to the world's greatest port, one needed sound knowledge of land rather than sea. For the Thames entrance is strewn with sandbanks, which for centuries have proved a hazard to shipping. Indeed the first lightship ever was placed at the Nore and by 1890 one T H Tizard reported in 'Nature' magazine that the Thames Estuary had "3 lighthouses, 11 light vessels, 8 gas buoys, 10 beacons, and 117 ordinary buoys". Yet this was not enough: "The demand for additional marks is likely to increase rather than diminish, for the deepest channels through the estuary have not yet been buoyed."

These same sandbanks, however, could provide salvation for many smaller craft. Thames sailing barges had for years found themselves anchored in flat, albeit hissing, water on the lee side of a sand while over to windward, perhaps not half a mile away, combers boomed through the gale.

It was an ambiguous place in which to sail and it produced an enigmatic sailor.

The young Maurice was learning the highway code of the Thames Estuary, sandbank by sandbank. His next grounding was on the Buxey. Heavy rain had obscured his visibility as he sailed *Vahan* up the Raysand Channel bound for the Crouch. The ebb was away and Maurice anxiously peered through the curtains of North Sea rain for a sight of the Buxey beacon.

"But no beacon appeared, while the seas became a little steeper and more sandy looking, and one angry little wave suddenly broke alongside and curled along the lee deck. Almost at the same instant I felt that sickening shock under me as the keel struck the sand. *Dabchick* rose on the next sea, surged onward; then as the swell raced ahead of her and her stern dropped, there was that shuddering bump again. Once more, lift, rush forward, then thud on the hard sand, almost jerking me off my feet."

Maurice padded across the hard back of the Buxey and found the beacon to starboard of his course. The ebb tide set across the sand to the east, not directly down the Raysand Channel as he had logically assumed. Now the cabin, which had given him a feeling of such warmth and homeliness that he would "not have changed places with any man in

England", was a "grotesque little world" with its crazy angles; a world compensated for only with the assistance of thick slices of bread and jam.

Although the sea had shrunk away this was its territory. For a few hours Maurice could plod in perfect safety on almost dry land. There would be no way of getting ashore proper, however, for then the Raysand, or Rays'n as everyone calls it, did not dry out but had water through it at all states of the tide, cutting off the Buxey from the Essex coast and leaving it a low tide island.

So there he sat, high and dry and safe and sound ... until the tide returned. Should it come back with an easterly gale, no longer would the Buxey be safe, but instead would shatter *Vahan* as she tried to float, leaving her master to drown.

Nervously Maurice waited:

"The sun was shedding a fiery red glow through the clouds as it set behind the distant hills, and all too soon night began to darken the ridged sand all around. The wind continued its moaning notes through the yacht's rigging, but at least one consolation was that the rain had stopped. I was still anxious to know how my boat would fare before she lifted and floated off, for I was aware of a continuous sound in the air, a muffled roaring like that of a train passing over a very long girder bridge, but seemingly far away, and I realised it was the seas breaking along the edge of the sands as the tide made again.

"The sound sent cold shivers down my spine, an intense feeling of loneliness swept over me, and I would have given anything to have one of my chums with me now ..."

Maurice, however, had become in his own words a "natural singlehander" for girls didn't interest him much - except as "puzzling rivals to boats". He had taken two sisters, friends of the family, out once but they seemed to him such "silly, shrill creatures with little boat sense that I preferred to sail alone".

He could not afford flares and considered soaking his bedding in paraffin, but realised he would never be seen - the nearest civilisation was Brightlingsea. No eye there would spot a flicker far out in the blackness.

Vahan did take a hammering as she refloated and Maurice sailed her through the night back to the safety of Harwich, but he had to sail and pump all the way as the old boat's rotten garboards had opened up, a fact he discovered next day when he beached her at Cann's bargeyard in Harwich.

It was time for another boat.

4

Ashore on the Gunfleet

The sailing season was over. As Maurice waited on the pebble hard at Pin Mill for his shipmate to turn up, he idly gazed at the red-leaded bottoms of the deep-keeled boats, while their owners tugged tarpaulins over them for the winter. It was late in the year for a coastal passage, he thought.

The sun was rapidly losing its grip on illuminating the darkening river Orwell. Out on the tide sat the long, low-sided hull of *Albatross* looking distinctly uninviting in the fading late autumn light. The wind rustled through the wooded cliffs above the hamlet. It sounded high. It would be stronger clear of Harwich ... 'Ting-a-ling,' a bicycle bell broke Maurice's reverie.

The burly form of Henry 'Morty' Mortimore dropped to one leg and dismounted. Even in the growing chill air the ruddy red face of Maurice's yachting partner was perspiring.

"Come on Griff," he said. "Quick as you like. Let's get underway."

The irrepressible Morty had just travelled all the way from Ware in Hertfordshire where he was chief clerk to the Midland Bank - which in 1922 did not close on a Saturday until 1 pm. As soon as it did, Morty, by bicycle and train, made his way across country to Pin Mill and his beloved *Albatross*.

On this particular Saturday the pair were bound for West Mersea where *Albatross* herself was to be laid-up. Maurice had sold *Vahan* and she had sailed away to the Thames. While he searched for another shoal draught yacht he had agreed to join Morty in a half share of *Albatross*, a Nore One Design. Several of these 22ft centreboarders had been built to race on the Thames along the Southend shore. The fact that they had been constructed with a miserable cuddy was enough for Morty to convince himself he had a proper cruiser rather than a day-racer with a wind-break!

At the Naze, with four hours of ebb left to punch and a

freshening sou'westerly wind, *Albatross*, already reefed, plunged headlong into seas with dimensions masked by the blackness of the night.

Miles away to windward the dancing fairy lights of Clacton flickered over wet, empty, end-of-season streets. The glow they sent up into the wild and windy night was an intermittent arc of orange to the crew of *Albatross* as the longshore one design struggled to the summit of and fell down between the waves.

A sudden squall pressed *Albatross*'s lee rail further under water and started a seam in her mainsail. The crew reacted swiftly and covered up the rent with two further rolls of tired sail around the boom.

Morty shouted instructions to Maurice from the coachroof as he reefed: "Better keep over to the Gunfleet side, we might get a bit of lee off the sands."

The Gunfleet has a long tail. Towards that *Albatross* lurched on as she vainly sought relief from the pounding seas.

The next crisis came as Morty realised a wave had smashed through the portlight in the forward end of the cabin coaming. He yelled at Maurice who dashed into the cabin and plugged the hole with a sodden cushion. The lee berth was awash and seawater sloshed round his ankles.

"I crawled into the cramped fo'c'sle, where the pounding sounded like thunder, and struck a match. The seams were working and water was trickling in here and there; I hoped, as the match went out, that the broken portlight was responsible for most of the bilge water."

Once again there was no time to light the cabin lamp. Almost as disheartening as their meteorological foe was the state of their refuge from it:

"It was a pity, however, that the only way we hoped to keep our blankets dry aboard this pitiful boat, by strapping them in a bundle over the table, had proved useless. All the bedding was by now soaked with saltwater."

Albatross blundered on blindly towards the Gunfleet as her crew searched in vain for that "lee". She was now perilously close and on a falling tide. When the inevitable happened Maurice frantically wound up the centreplate, but before Morty could get her about she struck the hard back of the sand again, this time with her keel.

As the sails flogged madly, their sheets whipping into the seas, the crew prepared the kedge anchor to be rowed off back out towards the Wallet. Maurice pulled in the painter - it was remarkably light - and found himself staring at a frayed end.

The dinghy had gone.

In another hour the seas had ebbed away and that eerie feeling of false security fell upon the two sole occupants of a temporary island.

They took solace in mugs of Oxo and the faithful Primus stove heated the sodden cabin into a clammy sauna-like cell.

Maurice was worried about Morty's appearance. All the bounce seemed to have gone out of his normally enthusiastic face.

"He looked very gaunt and rather waffled in his speech," Maurice recalls. "I thought 'Godfathers he's going crazy'. Then I realised the poor chap had taken his teeth out!"

Out on the seaward side of the Gunfleet the red 'eye' of the old screw pile lighthouse gave them a wink of seven seconds and blinked off for 23, its warning of danger to mariners appearing to mock the crew of *Albatross*.

To improve circulation, the pair - Morty at 40, was then 20 years Maurice's senior - went for a run across the windy sands. They splashed through puddles in the dark. Then it was back to the damp cabin, where they huddled on the sidebenches, for the little racer had no bunks, and boiled up further mugs of Oxo to fight off the apprehension they felt as the tide crept back in.

Nearly 70 years later, Maurice said:

"We were just damned careless that night. We took little notice of tides. We beat against the ebb and we stood too long on the starboard tack over the Gunfleet sands and we went aground. Now you would send up flares, you'd have the lifeboat out. We didn't have flares and everything was so wet. I think we came close then to losing the boat and, of course, with no dinghy, losing ourselves."

In his written account of *Albatross*'s dilemma Maurice considers the nearest civilisation to them, that of the Gunfleet lighthouse.

"The red flash of the Gunfleet lighthouse, standing on piles on the outer edge of the sands some four miles away, was clearly visible, and a flare would probably have attracted attention, or even brought the Clacton lifeboat out. But there was nothing dry enough at present to burn aboard for a flare..."

At that time the Gunfleet lighthouse, well described by Maurice as looking like a "water-tower on stilts", was manned by two men. It was also connected to the shore by a telegraph "for life saving purposes only" as the Admiralty List of Lights dictated.

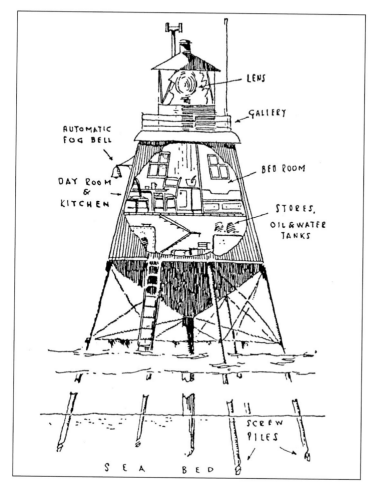

A typical pile lighthouse like the Gunfleet light

As the tide returned, *Albatross* took a severe pounding on those far offshore sands. Maurice and Morty took turns to check the timbers and seams by candlelight - they were convinced she would spring apart. As it was she floated, turned and they hauled her off through the combers on the kedge warp until it parted.

"Almost before I cried out, *Albatross* had been carried to leeward, and once more she slewed round and lay pounding on the sands. My heart sank, as it seemed for a moment as though we were doomed now; but, as fortune would have it, when she struck, the little boat had turned round to starboard, and she now lay with her bowsprit pointing towards Clacton lights - and the deep water of the Wallet."

They got her off and sailed to Mersea. Any smacksman up and about early in the Quarters that morning would have known the *Albatross* had taken some weather for the tanned mainsail was stained white with salt halfway up the cloths.

After Maurice told me about the grounding of *Albatross* I felt an irresistible desire to visit the sandbank which so nearly robbed the East Coast of its greatest yachtsman.

One February day I set off aboard *Sea Boots* a modern GRP 25-footer owned by a friend and colleague, Tim Cornall.

As we crept away from his berth at Bradwell and nosed out into early morning fog he was still trying to sell me a visit to Brightlingsea instead. Who on earth wanted to go and gaze at a sandbank? Well, that's the effect Maurice has and I knew that really Tim was internally trying to explain his own feeling of seduction.

We took a course through the Spitway and along the southern side of the Gunfleet in the East Swin. Tim was first

The Gunfleet Lighthouse today

to spot the lighthouse and handed me the binoculars. An eerie, whitish patchiness loomed through the fog. An inverted cupola stood suspended above the sea - its spidery legs still cut off in fog. The whiteness was explained as we steered in closer - I counted 12 cormorants as they shook their funereal shoulders and lifted reluctantly from the upper-works.

The davits from which the lighthouse keepers' skiff would have dangled, still curved over the sea. The windows of their home had been punched out by storms and left open to the damp sea air. The "red eye" of the light itself had gone, only the wrought iron railings around the summit being left to tell of its existence. They were provided to prevent the keepers being blown into the North Sea while outside swabbing off the salt from the glass casing. A south cardinal buoy now marks the head of the Gunfleet. The old lighthouse is derelict. It was erected and operational from 1856, replacing a lightvessel, and the light was finally extinguished in October 1939 as part of the wartime blackout, never to be re-lit.

The Gunfleet is shaped like a crooked old walking stick, the handle of which is almost severed at the neck by sea. It was this narrow strip of sand that we attempted to cross in *Sea Boots* in order to sail back up the Wallet on the lee side of the sand - a wise thing to do with a freshening southerly threatening to veer to the sou'west and strengthen further.

Just like Maurice we were attempting to get some lee from the sand. Unlike him though we had the luxury of an engine, a depth sounder and push button navigation systems.

We edged *Sea Boots* further and further into the brown water. We had decided to reverse at a sounding of 6ft (Sea Boots draws 3.5ft), which we changed to five when six came up more quickly than we had reckoned.

A seal surfaced not a mackerel throw from us, the cockpit depth recorder showed 4.3 feet and we backed off and instead skirted round the top edge of the walking stick's "handle" into the Wallet and safety once more. How near, I thought, Maurice had come to leaving us the bones of *Albatross* to search for.

His own experience on those ship-breaking sands had Maurice concluding: "...we blessed the coming of the day, for it meant that what was, we hoped, the worst night of our lives, was over."

Albatross was sold. Morty bought himself a large yawl and moved to Devon where there were no sandbanks, while Maurice remounted his bicycle and went in search of another shoal draught boat.

5

The Lifting Bridge

The little wooded valley, which drops gently down on the west bank of the River Orwell and stops abruptly at the water's edge with the 'Butt & Oyster' tavern, was first noticed by Maurice from the decks of the paddle steamers on which he journeyed with his parents to and from Harwich.

It was at Pin Mill that he found *Kitten*. She was up on blocks outside Harry King's yard and looked ill. The 24-footer's carvel planking was desperately in need of a drink, but Maurice liked the fact that she was a centreboarder with a lifting rudder. With both plates wound up she would float in 2ft of water. The "overgrown dinghy", as he described her, had been built as *Nellie* in 1906 by George Cardnell at Maylandsea in Essex.

She was an unusual construction being double skinned, with diagonal planking as the lining and the topside planking running horizontally. The £140 asking price was almost double Maurice's £80 spending money, but when he found out that the owners had already bought another craft he thought it worth a cheeky offer. His hopes were raised further on meeting the husband and wife team who sailed her. They were both over 6ft and Maurice felt that talking to them was like having a conversation with "people on horseback". *Kitten* was far too uncomfortable for them, luckily for Maurice, who in a tough barter batted them down to £65.

Once again Maurice threw seamanlike superstition to the wind and changed her name from Kitten, which he felt would be a name embarrassing to hail as well as to hear hailed. Remembering a line from Kipling's 'The Cat That Walked By Himself' - "by his own wild lone" - it was *Wild Lone* she became.

Harry King was a respected shipwright of the old school and not a glorified chandlers and brokerage as so many yards later became. As a result he did not hold boat owners captive, barring them from employing anyone other than his own yard

hands from working on their vessels.

When Maurice had *Wild Lone* ready to launch, the whole yard turned out to help with her rigging and Harry's crane was used at no extra cost to step her mast. When Maurice nervously enquired as to his bill he was told to flood the bar of the 'Butt' with beer.

Maurice toasted Harry's helpful crew as he looked proudly through the bar window at *Wild Lone* floating on the top of the tide a stone's throw from the pub.

"... I confess it was the jolliest launching I ever attended."

It was in the ownership of *Wild Lone* that Maurice began to compare notes. Something was telling him it would be useful in future days to observe the vices and virtues of different types of hull and rig. He started making lists of his observations. He was becoming a pundit.

Of *Wild Lone* he was later to write: "This type of boat with a flat floor amidships, like a dinghy, is a holy terror for rolling. Having great initial stability her hull endeavours to remain upright to the surface of the water, and as a swell passes beneath her she rolls in quick, dizzy arcs. The deep-keeled yacht, on the other hand, seldom rolls noticeably, but lifts up and down and plunges. Having very little initial stability she does not tend to fall on her side as the sloping face of a wave approaches her, but lifts bodily to the swell."

Fortunately Maurice did not sacrifice his quaint accounts

Wild Lone
(ex Kitten,
ex Nellie*)*
24´x22´x8.2´x2´
ex CB, 1923.
*(Built by Geo
Cardnell, 1906)*

of East Coast voyaging for the cold prose of the technician and he continued to give us his delightful accounts of explorations with *Wild Lone*, such as his first passage through the mysterious strait of Havengore.

This isolated and spooky back double takes the ditch crawling yachtsman behind the sedge grass of Foulness Island, avoiding the sea route through the Swin.

A low lying delta of marshy islands, it has two factors that give it its eerie charm. One is that the whole archipelago is reclaimed land and so low is it one feels it really still belongs to the sea. The other is that much of the territory is owned by the Ministry of Defence who guard its military secrets jealously. Anyone wishing to visit the island or its pub, the 'George & Dragon' - there used to be two until the 'King's Head' closed some years ago - has to pre-arrange his arrival with the landlord who will then telephone the MOD police checkpoint at the entrance to the island. If your car registration and your name tallies you are allowed on. The yachtsman has a more powerful right of passage. Old by-laws give him right of way through the Havengore Bridge at tide time and the military are obliged to lift the bridge for him.

It is the same for pedestrians - ancient rights of way allow him access to the Broomway, a path that runs some three miles or more across the Maplin Sands from Wakering Stairs to Fisherman's Head on Foulness itself. Anyone ringing to ask for the permission they don't require will be scared off with warnings of unexploded shells dotted along the roadway, which runs across the ranges and is of course covered at high water.

Havengore and its environs are the same today as they were in 1923 when Maurice first sailed them: "... we turned off to port and found ourselves hurrying along the narrowest and most winding little creek that I had ever sailed in. At one point our boom end rustled through the long sedge grass on the high bank to leeward, while a good yard or so to windward the water grew agitated at the edge of the mud as we approached, receded a few inches as we swept past and then joined the series of little short waves that followed from our quarter and ran, curling and chuckling, up the slope of the mud."

In my old yacht *Almita* I have negotiated the Narrow Cut several times. Once, having sailed through the Havengore Bridge, we met the full force of a spring flood which, having covered the wide expanse of the Maplin and dropped a couple of feet over the Broomway bar, was gushing into the creek itself at an alarming rate of knots. We lost the wind, blanketed by the raised bridge, and were flung round broadside and pinned by the tide to the girders.

A few longshorefolk gathered round, spread their elbows on the railings just above us and watched, rather like pedestrians around a road excavation.

"You wanna get an oar on it, mate," said one helpful observer to my crew, Tim, who had the veins on his forehead raised by his efforts at trying to push us clear.

"It's a bloody cart horse we need not an oar," Tim replied.

We eventually hauled *Almita* clear with a kedge anchor.

My father, the late Richard Stephens Durham, sailed down Narrow Cuts in his Utility One Design, *Sprite*, about 10 years after Maurice's first visit. An 18ft, threequarter-decked dayboat, *Sprite* was no boat to sleep on, especially nearing Christmas, so when the weather proved too rough for him and his crew to leave the safety of Havengore Creek, they asked the bridge keeper if he would keep an eye on the moored dayboat while they caught a bus home. It was late in the day, already near dusk and the bridge keeper insisted the young lads sat and ate a roast dinner with him and his wife, then spend the night in their cottage. It saved father a trip to and from the boat and they were able to leave the following morning when the weather had improved.

Maurice, too, had found the bridge keeper a personable fellow:

"We came to the iron bridge that connects Foulness to the mainland near Shoeburyness, and were surprised to find it raised for us to pass through. As *Wild Lone* slid under the black underside of the bridge, and her wash echoed amongst the girders above, a man leant out of the control house and cupped his hands.

"'You'd better bring up just below, sir. There ain't enough water over the bar yet.'"

They soon befriended the bridgeman and all three looked out towards the Maplin over which the flood was creeping.

Far away in the river, "London's shipping, hull down and faint, was converging from the four corners of the earth."

Bewitched by the place, Maurice and his crew decided to skip the next tide and spend the night in Havengore.

"That night Wild Lone took the ground when the water had run out of the creek, and three miles of level, yellow sand separated her from the Thames - the strange mysterious Maplins...

"For a long time we sat smoking in the well, listening to

the faint murmur of the retreating tide on the sands outside, and the sudden cry of wild-fowl that took to invisible flight in the night air."

The following day after a thrash across the estuary, *Wild Lone* anchored in the peace and quiet of Stangate Creek near the hamlet of Halstow at the creek's head.

In *Wild Lone* Maurice experienced a broken gooseneck and the centreplate chain parting, both of which would garner future advice for yachtsmen reading his copy.

At the end of the season he sold *Wild Lone* and she sailed away to an unsuitable new port somewhere on the south coast.

Before the year was out Maurice was to spend another night off Foulness, this time not in the security of Havengore Creek, but out on the back of the exposed Maplins themselves.

He was making a passage from Mersea to Westcliff-on-Sea aboard the barge yacht *Curlew*, later owned by my father in the 1950s and kept at the collection of ancient lighters in Leigh Creek, which marked Les Warland's yard.

While halfway up Swin, beating against a fresh sou'westerly the bolt holding the starboard leeboard to the boat's topside sheered off. Immediately her skipper, Barney, who was taking her back to the Southend shore to lay her up, steered landwards.

"It was almost dark now and difficult to make out even the distant sea wall on Foulness Island, but the white crests flashed across the intervening miles like green fire. And as Curlew bustled into the gathering night the Swin seas gave way to the Maplin choppiness and we knew we were over the sands...

"With anchor down and sails stowed *Curlew* lay rising and falling over the seas as she tugged at her cable on the first of the lee-going ebb. And as the water fell lower even these little seas died down, and by the time we had cooked and eaten a late meal all motion had ceased, and *Curlew* sat solidly on the sand with her short mast as upright as a gate post.

"The night was cold and we wore our seaboots when we stepped overboard on to the wet sand which was ridged from the tide and as hard as a pavement."

They soon had a new bolt fitted and by the time they were finished: "All sign of the sea had receded into the night leaving miles of bare sand, and only a distant roar along the edge of the sands came to remind us of the boisterous element we had been recently fighting." Maurice was impressed. Here was a boat which sat up like a house on the sand, which would float on a "heavy dew" and therefore be off the bottom before the seas could reach ship-breaking proportions. Not only that, she had a roomy cabin too.

"As we turned into our bunks for a few hours' welcome sleep ... some of the benefits of a flat-bottomed barge yacht were forcibly impressed on me: here we were, quite still and quiet, upright and comfortable and unmoved by the restlessness of the sea that came to us as a continuous murmur from miles away."

Approaching the old Havengore Bridge

6

The Backwaters

A humble box, pointed at one end, with lifting fan-shaped fulcrums on either side was considered worthy enough to display for scientific posterity, E B Tredwen, pioneer of the barge yacht, has to this day a model of his craft *Doreen* at the Kensington Science Museum.

It was now to the barge-yacht that Maurice turned. Before 1923 was over he had bought *Swan*, built in 1897 by Burgoine at Chiswick. With a 17in draught she was the shallowest boat he ever owned. Her 26ft lengths of planking were without timbers; instead she had stringers running fore and aft. Even more unusual was the fact that her leeboards were internal.

The next weekend available, Maurice set off for the first time in *Swan*. He soon learnt there was a price to pay for such a minimal draught. Though there was a fresh sou'westerly blowing he had got used to *Wild Lone*'s seaworthy qualities and therefore did not take in a reef.

"A few minutes later a puff came from over the trees below Pin Mill and I received a severe fright. *Swan* suddenly heeled right over with the water up to her lee rail and her weather chine at least 2ft out of the water. I felt the little waves thump under her flat bottom amidships as I scrambled up on the weather coaming, and pushed the helm down with my foot. The boat swung round head to wind, still lying over at this crazy angle, until the sails were ashake. It seemed inevitable that she should fall over on her side; then suddenly she righted, the chine came down on the water with a heavy thump and in a flash she was round on the other tack, racing back up-river with her foresail backed!"

Maurice immediately pulled down two reefs, but even then he found she had to be treated like a sailing dinghy.

"As soon as I left the helm she charged off on one tack, swung up into the wind, and then paid right off with the foresail aback, until she had the wind on her quarter. Then she heeled over until my mouth became dry with apprehension, tore round once more in a wide sweep, and went about again on the other tack. There seemed to be something devilish about this, as though the boat were throwing a fit!"

Maurice went even further when he told me of *Swan*'s tenderness:

"She was very unstable, very narrow in the beam, there was no ballast in her, no keel; there were just these two very heavy plates. She capsized twice before I bought her. She was being raced off Heybridge and turned over quite easily. She didn't sink, she floated with air trapped under the weather deck and rather like the modern dinghies they were able to get her back up again.

"I had her up on her ear far too often for my liking. I realised she wasn't anything like as good a boat as *Wild Lone*. It was rather sad, a silly thing to do.

"However, sometimes she was quite a joy to sail."

Indeed she was. That first time on the Orwell, Maurice, having 'broken her in', went slashing past two friends in much longer boats. That night in the 'Butt' they expressed their disgust at being overhauled by a box.

In Harwich harbour *Swan*, even reefed, did nothing to reassure her owner. He put the helm over and sailed back rather crestfallen to Pin Mill, where Maurice now kept a mooring, since Ipswich dock had been extended into The Bight.

Yet again Maurice had been seduced by a cabin: "... with a clean, well equipped cabin, all fitted in polished mahogany,

Swan, *27ft*
1923
(Built at
Hampton-on-
Thames, 1897)

spring bunks (a luxury I had so far not experienced) ...."

By now he was consciously making copious notes on the different boats he bought and sold. Further experience of different craft he gleaned through his yacht brokerage. Much of his writing now had the direction of a book on the practical aspects of yachting. Yet Maurice was to make himself a legend through his evocative accounts of local voyaging. It was his ability to take readers with him on passage that was later to give him such enormously wide appeal.

We have the floating study that was *Swan* to thank for inspiring Maurice to bring us the charm of the marshy Essex creeks so often overlooked and never before captured so vividly.

What has to be Maurice at his best is the chapter entitled 'The Silent Creeks' in 'The Magic of the Swatchways', which was taken down in note form in the tail end of 1923, many years before the book was published.

Maurice was beginning to enjoy his small shoal cruisers, for in them he could sail alone - obviously a necessity for a writer - and in them he could nose far up some lonely creek to an isolated anchorage for the silence that lured out the magic.

One can picture this wise young man thrashing to windward out of Harwich harbour aboard *Swan* as a friend passes in his magnificent deep yacht and shouts: "You'll have her over if you aren't damn careful."

Maurice smiles to himself at the superior arrogance of such a hail. He gives a diffident wave, then turns back to face the sou'wester, but "The words floated down to me as the distance between us rapidly increased, but I caught the note of scorn that told of an inborn hatred of barge yachts and of consolation for fools who drive about in them ..."

Soon the Pye Sand had its arm round the hard-pressed *Swan*. In the flat water she cut along happily with no seas to punch her exposed chine.

Here I hope the reader will forgive me for running a full excerpt from 'The Silent Creeks', but the tour around that muddy Essex paradise - the Walton Backwaters - was discovered by Maurice and his typewriter long before Arthur Ransome got there and fixed the place for his book *Secret Water*.

"*Swan* appeared relieved at the sudden change, and as she heeled again to a last mild gust she whisked up Hamford Water while the red buoy at the mouth of Walton Creek bubbled past, nodding his beweeded head as if to say, 'Oh, all right. Don't come up here if you don't want to!' And the row of withies that stood against the edge of Horsey Island waved to us as though they themselves were surprised that any self-respecting yacht should prefer to go up Hamford Water for the night instead of the more congenial surroundings of the Twizzle and Walton itself.

"The only beacon that remained neutral was the dear old thing with the can set jauntily on his head. I like that beacon. He is the one I usually run into when trying to make Walton Creek on a dark night. A canny withy, indeed, which has suffered much!

"But tonight I wanted solitude. The Twizzle, with its small crowd of yachts, the dinghies flitting here and there with vociferously happy crews; the congenial club house, with its crowded rooms and laughter and smoke-filled bar; the ladies' room with its chattering occupants that seemed to all the world like a poultry run wherein a terrier has been let loose and the streets and 'prom' of the 'attractive watering-place' itself ... No. Tonight I had a lot of writing to do, and it was one of those pitifully rare occasions when the so-called 'urge to write' did not require to be dragged forth by the scruff of its unwilling neck and compelled by mental cudgelling to produce, produce and then some.

"The sedge-covered flats of Horsey Island were slipping by close to windward, and the lonely cries of wildfowl were carried across them by the dying breeze. Once a flock of redshank sailed across our bows on a level with the burgee, the swish of their wings passing like a gentle whisper in the trees. And Kirby Creek opened out, revealed itself abeam, then closed up once more and passed astern; just an opening in the sedge bank wherein one saw a twisting stream of water leading to - where? One could imagine it as a smugglers' haunt that became the scene of silent grim activity on dark nights."

Next came Pewit Island "with its deserted, winding creek leading in towards the dim hills that stood on the mainland past the quaint factory that seems almost derelict, passed astern gradually, and before us Hamford Water broke up into two narrow channels."

Maurice and *Swan* skate easily onward even over the now fast-running ebb.

"On either side the mud was revealing itself in naked simplicity, and a continuous hiss came from it as the tide receded; whilst here and there little jets of water spurted up where tiny creatures lived and throve. Then the idea of the little terrier let loose amongst the hens recurred, and my thoughts reverted, in some mysterious fashion, to the congenial club house but two miles away ..."

Maurice, only 21, resisted the lure of wine, women and song however and stuck determinedly to his course.

"The sun had just set behind vague clouds that had refused him one last look at the world before retiring for the night, and darkness was waiting to descend upon us. The autumn air was chilly now, and I beat my hands to restore their vanished circulation. Across a level bank of mud the trees on Skipper's Island were silhouetted against the darkening sky in the east. They stood clustered together as though afraid of the oncoming gloom, gaunt arms spread out towards one another, heads nodding sleepily, the grass at their feet already drowsy and inert. A faint air passed through their still branches, and their sigh came delicately across the intervening mud and water, a sigh of contentment that a child makes when it is on the verge of Dreamland."

A rumble from the bilges broke Maurice's reverie and he hurriedly hauled up the leeboards.

"At last the tiny creek that led between the two islets appeared to starboard, and in a minute the slim little barge was chuckling up between two steep banks that closed in upon her until there seemed not room to pass another vessel of her size, should we meet one. But the chance was unlikely, for few cabin yachts get up as far as this, except at high water, and no open boats would be about here at this time in the evening. The place seemed utterly deserted, and as the rugged outline of the banks on either side slid silently by I could not help thinking what an ideal place it would be to ambush a visiting yacht and hold her to ransom ... Once a number of fowl took to the air from the grass close to leeward, and their sudden advent startled me as though a rifle bullet had passed through my mainsail!

"As quickly as it had narrowed the creek opened out again, and revealed before me a dim expanse of water on which ripples chased one another amongst tall grass that appeared here and there above the placid surface. It was now too dark to see the quay at the head of the creek, but one or two lights told where the cottages that looked over the water at high tide stood near the wharf. There is a faint channel that leads right up to Beaumont's Quay, but I did not know it, and although I saw one stray withy apparently out in the middle I knew not which side of it the deeper water lay."

The leeboards started ploughing the bottom again and Maurice looked about him:

"Hardly a sound broke the stillness of the oncoming night. The wind had almost died right away, and only when a cat's paw kissed the tanned mainsail did the dinghy reveal its presence by murmuring contentedly. I looked back at my wake. It was smooth off the weather quarter, and a line of bubbles was rising to the surface from under the rudder. We were making frightful leeway.

"Then she stopped. It was no use trying to get any nearer the quay now. She was aground for the night. So was the dinghy. Never mind, it was quite a nice place, and, being a barge, she would sit upright. I jumped over in my sea boots into a few inches of water and planted the anchor a few yards away. Then the canvas was stowed and everything on deck made shipshape.

"It was quite dark now, and while the Primus stoves were left to boil water and heat up a typical stew, and the light from the little corner cabin lamp cast beams through the rectangular portlights, I sat on the cabin-top and listened to the sounds of the night.

"A train was pulling out from Frinton Station. A dog heard it and barked. A curlew, from somewhere over Skipper's Island, called his mate and got no reply. Wrong number or wrong mate. Voices were coming faintly from the direction of the quay, and a motorhorn broke the stillness of the Kirby road. And the mud all round was hissing as the last of the tide receded from sight, leaving a thin, tortuous rivulet that trickled down the middle of the creek a few feet from the yacht's bow.

"The night grew colder as the stars appeared one by one, and above the uncertain marshes through which we had threaded our way a mist was rising, ghostlike, unfolding its white coils over the damp grass and making the scene vaguer and more mysterious than ever."

Maurice sought the warmth of his cabin, ate his stew, then turned up the oil lamp. The patter of his typewriter carried over the marshes like invisible tracer fire. A screech owl answered back.

"But what a change next morning! The early sun, glad to be about again, was glinting on the dew-covered deck, and what had been the previous night murky stretches of uncertain mud was now an expanse of mirror-like water. Hardly a breath stirred, and the reflections of the trees were reproduced faithfully on the placid surface. From the wharf a barge was drifting down, light, her familiar topsail and big mainsail set in the hope of catching any draught that was going. It was just high water, and the islands that had last night appeared as high banks of mud with gaunt sedge on the top, now seemed to be flat fields of coarse grass out of which grew lonely rotten stumps and broken withies.

"The barge drifted nearer, her reflection playing idly before the bluff bows, and her dinghy following on the end of a heavy painter that drooped in the middle to the surface. As the stately old vessel glided past within a few yards of *Swan*, the old skipper left the wheel and stood against the rail, hands in pockets, surveying the unfamiliar little barge yacht."

The two skippers exchange pleasantries as the obligatory barge dog runs yapping insanely back and forth along the deck.

"And when they had gone and only the masts and patched tanned sails appeared over the sedge grass of the unnamed islet, I stripped in the well, paused for a deep breath on the cabin-top, and then dived into the limpid depths of the creek. And everywhere silence reigned, the silence of big open spaces, of Nature at her best, of the creeks."

Swan
*Paul, and son
Toby Lester,
Leigh 1981*

7

A Warm Cabin

Ablanket of snow covered every feature of the boat's decks except amidships where a watery, rusty circle surrounded the smoking chimney. Down below a "Jack Tar" coal-stove glowed red and "was reflected in soft light on the bulkhead, the row of books in their shelf, and in the varnished skylight. It reflected also as a square of bright light on the polished brass of the gimballed bulkhead lamp, adding to its own warm glow, for evening was already upon us."

Maurice had found the best cabin yet. *Swan* he had sold to a family until then used only to sailing dinghies. His next boat, *Storm*, was built at Leigh-on-Sea in 1910 on the lines of that port's most famous craft, the bawley. Not surprisingly she came off the ways at Bundock's Yard where many of her bigger working sisters had been built. She was 25ft overall with a 9ft beam and drawing 3ft 3in, full enough in the midship section to sit upright on the mud yet with enough keel to keep her cutter rig stiff to windward in a blow. "To

Storm, 1924 (My favourite ship till that time. Built by Bundock Bros, Leigh-on-Sea, 1910)

me then she was the ideal boat," Maurice told me.

Maurice floated her off a berth in the marshes at Mersea and soon had her rigged out for some late winter sailing in 1924. She was the first vessel he had owned with an engine, in this case a 3 ½ horsepower Kelvin.

It was as well *Storm* had such a comfortable cabin as her skipper spent many more evenings aboard when cruising than he did ashore. Whether he was singlehanded and needed to write, or with a crew, Maurice was not among the yachtsmen who will pull a boat several miles against the ebb to make a pint in some raucous pub.

A night aboard would include the ritual evening meal cooked on the coal stove, in the case of *Storm*, and the trusty Primus in his earlier yachts. Then with perhaps a bottle of brown ale it was feet up on the locker for both skipper and crew and a good book.

Such simple resourcefulness was as well for after one cruise down the Medway and round the Swale, *Storm*

Storm *loved a strong, fair wind*

brought up in the East Swale in preparation for the next leg - home across the estuary. But a sou'westerly gale dragged the boat down river towards the huge whale-backed mud bank which almost divides the river in two below Faversham Creek. On the back of this *Storm* was to squat for 10 hours!

"... *Storm* had begun to drag her anchor. But we did not worry, for a hundred yards under our lee the soft mud of Horse Shoal was uncovering like a flat pudding, the little waves breaking furiously round the windward side, leaving a rim of white froth. *Storm* took the mud gently and ceased to drag. The waves broke impotently against her black bows for a little time, growing less fierce as the tide dropped; all movement in the old boat subsided, and slowly the little waves retreated, leaving us sitting in an expanse of flat mud over which froth was blown like down before the wind, while the gulls wheeled and planed over their feeding ground with weird devilish cries."

Maurice and his crew sat in the cockpit watching brailed barges shatter waves into spray far away out in the Thames beyond the other sands that muzzle the East Swale entrance. They stared at the large Whitstable smacks canted over on the hard sand off Shingle Street.

The sand of the Swale is really mud, so the shipmates could not relieve their long wait with a stroll on Horse Shoal. What provided a gooey cushion for *Storm* would be a suction cup hell for the sea-booted pedestrian.

They smoked cheroots. They watched a slab-sided motor cruiser thrash up the East Swale and anchor off Faversham Creek. They watched the crew row ashore leaving the motor-craft to sheer wildly around on her cable.

Maurice's mate, who kept a deep yacht on the Solent, haughtily dismissed the motor yacht as being something that would wreck the peace of a silent creek, perhaps in deference to his skipper.

And finally they sat and watched the tide make.

"The rising tide had crept round us now, and its edge was advancing in timid, furtive little rushes of animated froth, like ginger-beer, up the smooth slope of the mud. Like a well-trained army, it was advancing towards the middle of the shoal from all sides, and we knew it would meet and obliterate the highest mound in the middle as inevitably as the setting of the sun. The gulls knew it too, for they fought more and more savagely and scolded one another with raucous cries as their feeding ground became more and more restricted. The subdued waves were beating against our hull

(Above and
opposite)
Storm *as she
was in April
1930, in
Heybridge
Basin one cold
morning*

now with a plop, plop while little green crabs fought and
chased one another in and out of the advancing water.

"By the time the last stronghold of the doomed island was
overwhelmed and disappeared beneath the rising tide, *Storm*
had begun to show signs of awakening. The tiller moved
spasmodically as the water fussed round the rudder ..."

The wind had eased off but was still in the sou'west and
therefore a fair one for the passage home. Night was falling.
The crew was preparing what he thought would be supper
before hauling off into deeper water and turning in.

"I think this wind's going to last all night," said Maurice.
"It's always steady at night, and as it's a fair wind for us -
well what about it?"

The mate was pacified with the promise of hot food.

Once *Storm* was pushing the flood in the East Swale
channel, "It seemed as though the whole of the Thames were
rushing to meet us, and as it rolled over in a never-ending
turmoil of greeny phosphorescence, while drops leapt
forward and lit up the untroubled water ahead with tiny
splashes of light, like twinkling stars that raced to join the
curling wave.

"... As we left the mouth of the Swale astern not a single
light could be seen. It was swallowed up in the night as
though it had never existed. Even the dim riding light of the
little white motor cruiser was obscured now by Shellness
Point. To starboard the lights of Whitstable and Herne Bay
began to open out like the rows of portholes of a liner, while
as we drew abreast of Warden Point on the north shore of

Sheppey the loom of Southend, some 15 miles away, appeared like an unnatural dawn in the sky. None of the lights along the front or on the pier could be seen, however, for they would be below the horizon."

The whole estuary lay ahead of them and in its vast bay the miles of sand were marked by a pinball wizardry of winking, multi-coloured lights and among the ones that winked and flashed and flared were stealthy lights that marked hazards above the waves:

"...here and there the steady red or green lights between two equally steady white lights denoted the silent passage of a steamer through the night."

Once across the steamer track *Storm* passed the road signs of the Swin - Maplin lighthouse, Swin Middle light float and Wallet Spitway. By the time they were off Colne Point a grey, low-lying smudge marked earth breaking away from sky as day came.

For months now Maurice had been writing un-commissioned articles for newspapers and magazines in an attempt to supplement his yacht agency earnings, which were erratic.

But in *Storm* he was to become the subject of a news story himself.

While sailing through the Rays'n in half a gale of wind Maurice and crew spotted a barge-yacht, *Wavecrest of Leigh*, high and dry on Foulness Sand. Then to leeward of them they saw what they took to be the Buxey Beacon, but through the binoculars the beacon metamorphosed into a dinghy with a human aboard waving frantically.

They bore away towards the boat - a difficult and dangerous manoeuvre on a falling tide in heavy seas - to sail into shallower water.

After many attempts to get the dinghy in tow, gybing and tacking round the craft in ever decreasing depth, they eventually succeeded. Aboard were two lads dressed only in underpants.

They were soon wrapped up in *Storm*'s berths fast asleep with the faithful Oxo inside them and the coal stove radiating a reassuring glow while Maurice towed the craft into Mersea. The teenagers were from *Wavecrest*, which had run ashore on Foulness while trying to make the Crouch. As the crew tended to their anchor their dinghy painter parted and the elder of the two stripped off and swam off to it intending to row back. He couldn't manage it against the wind and tide so the other stripped off and joined him. They were blown away across the Crouch and over the Buxey sand and to heaven knows where if *Storm* had not spotted them.

At 22 years of age Maurice was a very contented yachtsman. He had owned five boats and *Storm*, his sixth, was the best, "like a favourite old black shoe" as he affectionately described her. Already he had gained immense experience about sailing and the qualities of different yachts. He had cruised just about all the creeks of the Thames Estuary. He had seen his words published in local newspapers - items on sailing, racing results from the local clubs, and pieces too on his first love, trains and railways.

And so might it all have continued in this way - the yacht agency making slow but steady growth, the articles eventually leading to a column on the 'East Anglian Daily Times'. And the world might not have heard of Maurice Griffiths.

But fate was to change all that.

8

Homeless

A large marquee in the garden of 10 Gippeswyk Avenue flapped in the wind coming up the Orwell valley. Its guy ropes flexed with each gust reminding Maurice painfully of *Storm*. He wondered covetously who was steering her at this moment, where she was bound ...

He had not sailed the boat a year before family circumstances had forced him to sell her. Now he watched as the nosy neighbours of Gippeswyk Avenue filed in through the front gate to have a good gander at "what Walter was worth".

His father had died suddenly of a heart attack one night before the end of 1924. Maurice carried with him forever the medical phrase describing his father's demise at the age of 52 - "ruptured aorta aneurism".

It was hardly surprising.

Without Walter's presence to bluff and muddle things along, the family discovered to their horror that he had been on the verge of bankruptcy. He owed money everywhere - to friends, to bookmakers, his bank; his mortgage instalments were in arrears and he even owed money to his employers, who had been regularly advancing him cash on his salary.

The bank foreclosed and the house was emptied of its contents, which were auctioned off in the marquee. Then the house itself was sold.

"My father, we thought, had been doing very nicely - we owned the house and everything, but we didn't see he was very unwise and he lost goodness knows how much on horse racing. He invested very badly and he was very nearly bankrupt - another year and I think he would have been. It was a dreadful thing in those days ... There was nothing at all. So we scattered," Maurice recalled.

Lena went to live with her married sister Sarah Trevis in Lincolnshire. Maurice managed to sell his yacht agency: "I sold the list - it wasn't a long one - to one of the other agents. We were glad of the money."

The money went towards Walter's debts and a penniless Maurice was left to decide whether to try for a job on the 'East Anglian Daily Times' - they had carried articles of his and his racing reports of the Orwell Sailing Club, which had now become the Orwell Yacht Club - or head back to the city of his birth and carve out a career as a journalist on the national newspapers. Either way he was never to use his middle name - where it was avoidable - again. It is Walter.

With just a few pounds in his pocket and the salt-stained portable typewriter he had carried aboard his boats, Maurice stood on the station at Ipswich and glanced up to the little red brick houses of Gippeswyk Avenue. He had decided on London.

Thus began the worst 10 months of his life.

"I moved around different bedsits in the Euston area. If the rent was too much I'd move on or if the bedsit was too bad I'd move on. Life revolved around a gas ring and a single room."

Maurice ate very little and the weight dropped off him as he batted away on the typewriter trying desperately to make ends meet. There were short stories for the London 'Evening' papers - the 'Standard' and the 'News'. They paid three guineas a time, but were difficult to break into. There were recipes half-remembered from flour and water efforts aboard *Storm* and the other boats, for 'Vogue' magazine. There were also thousands of words on every aspect of sailing that Maurice could produce for the yachting magazines.

He drew on all his youthful experience of yachting to provide copy.

There was a piece entitled 'Reflections on Smack Yachts' explaining the benefits of such craft, eg their low cost to keep up, handiness, low purchase price ... how the memory of *Storm* must have hurt!

Another called 'Reflections on Draught', in which the blessings, but also the shortfalls of barge-yachts are mentioned - all written on the same typewriter he kept aboard *Swan*.

There was even a piece about the virtues of 'Cementing Old Boats', in which he writes: "True, it (the cement) kept her bottom from dropping out - which after all, was an inconvenience avoided - but it didn't keep her from leaking. No, by gosh, I nearly wore that darned pump out, having to replace half the river every evening!" *Undine* was as fresh in his memory as ever. Maurice also used his imagination and ability to research a subject to produce even more articles.

There is a very curious humorous piece in which Maurice imagines a longboat with some high-born Danes visiting the Thames Estuary in 929 AD.

Olaf Wolfnoth the Buoyant writes in his log: "Thors Day. Sighted coast of Essex. Verily a fine view. Rounded Whittaker beacon." The steersman puts the ship called *Dragon* ashore on the Buxey.

"You see, they did it even in those days," Maurice wrote, remembering *Dabchick*'s stranding.

"I was pretty desperate as you can imagine," Maurice told me.

Yet all these articles were published.

There was a long piece on 'Dutch Yachts' - Maurice had yet to set foot in the low countries across the North Sea. It too found a publisher.

An American yachting paper - 'Fore An' Aft' - regularly employed Maurice's pen. As it was not published in the UK

Ex-fishing Botter Maartje. *Calm night on the Ijselmeer*

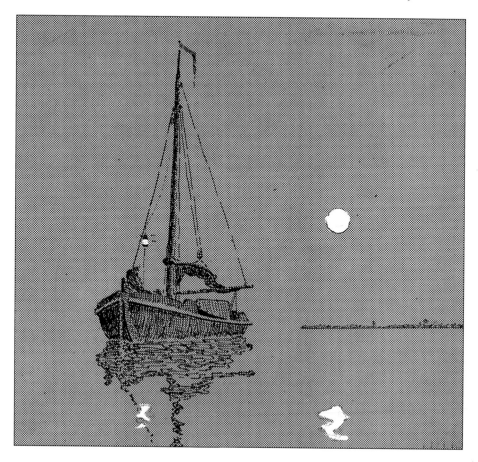

he was happy to hack away at rather more experimental nautical pieces.

Another, this one British, also took his copy. Called 'Yacht Owner' the magazine fired Maurice's enthusiasm. He felt he might get a break through the journal.

Consequently he turned out a lot of material for it. The trouble was their cheques never arrived.

"It was quite an attractive weekly and for the best part of a year I never got a penny. It was always a promise of when things get easier you'll get paid," a rueful Maurice remembers.

Things did not get easier though; instead the magazine folded and Maurice was never paid.

"It went out of circulation," said Maurice. "And it seemed an awful waste of time especially when I needed the money."

Maurice padded back to his Euston bedsit, shut the door and started a fresh article. Unlike his father, Maurice was not a big eater, nor did he carry excess weight; rather he took after his mother - a long, lean face with fine chiselled features. Now, however, friends who saw him were alarmed at the gauntness in his cheeks. They were not reassured either by the determined fire in his eyes. He started suffering from stomach cramps and the respiratory problems that had always dogged him worsened.

Deliverance was not far away however.

That first book Maurice had been compiling ever since *Wild Lone* days had been published in the spring of 1925. It was called 'Yachting On A Small Income' and a certain commuter, George Bittles, had bought a copy on the station platform one morning on his way to work as manager of a new yachting journal - 'Yacht Sales and Charters'.

Under the second chapter entitled 'What Will It Cost?' Mr Bittles became absorbed as he read the following:

"Public interest, such as it is, centres itself round the larger yacht races, and abundant photographs of big yachts with smart crews and white decks under a cloud of snowy canvas adorn the best papers in conjunction with art pictures of the latest things to be worn during the current yachting week. This suits public taste, but it throws the real phase of yachting, the core of the sport, into an obscure background, whither the listless eye of the public seldom penetrates.

"If you have sufficient of the 'needful' there is no reason whatever why you or your yacht should not brighten the pages of the best pictorials, if that be your ambition, but for you this book is not written. I assume that, with a 'little money in the bank', you want to be able to take health-giving, invigorating week-ends on the river and sea with the companionship of perhaps one or two kindred spirits. Then I think I can give you some idea of the probable cost of the sport followed with these ideals."

Mr Bittles read on unperturbed by the inky pages of broadsheet newspapers being rustled around him in the cramped commuter train. At a time when a brand new racing yacht cost between £100 and £150 a ton to build here was some chap telling him he could have a 20-footer for under £60 ... "and probably could be purchased judiciously for £30".

The book was sub-titled 'A Talk With "The Man In The Street"', which, in this case, was Mr George Bittles who went on to learn about the upkeep, rig, handling, even the insurance, of yachting on a shoe-string.

And, of course, there was a chapter on cabins.

"If you buy cutlery, get stainless knives. Ordinary steel knives insist on rusting ... buy crockery that isn't easily broken, large cups of good squat shape, and deep plates. Have racks with holes cut in them to take tumblers and sauce bottles, so that these do not fall over as the boat plunges into a head-sea while lying over at an angle of 35 degrees."

Mr Bittles read on. For cooking, the Primus, the author had concluded, was the best "stove" in a small boat. He did all his "frying" on a Primus with the "aid of an asbestos mat, which can be bought for about 2 and a half penny." Lighting was achieved with a gimballed oil lamp having its candlepower enhanced by using a "cheap mirror" behind the flame.

To make bunk cushions, a mattress from a 4ft 6in bed might be procured, which a "female relative might be induced to cut down the middle and cover the two halves with cretonne or something similar".

Mr Bittles was a man who had known nothing about boats. As a "man in the street" he now knew something about boats. By the time his train pulled into Waterloo Station he had decided on the man who should edit his new magazine.

Maurice recalls: "I had learnt about boats and I had wanted to write about them. After three boats I got the idea that there was a need for a simple book on how to go and buy a boat, also showing that you didn't have to be a wealthy man to do so. All the yachts, even in the Orwell, were much bigger than the things we were playing around in."

Suddenly Maurice was on a salary of £4 a week, in a warm

office, with his own desk.

"I had no money when George Bittles got in touch. He had
bought a political magazine called the 'Saturday Review' and
found this little thing about boats attached to it. He did say
that if my new direction didn't succeed, he would give up on
the magazine because it was losing too much money.

"It was really a Godsend," Maurice goes on. "He asked me
to come to his office and asked me if I was free. Was I free? I
took the job on the spot."

9

Peter Gerard

She was very slim and very pretty and made efforts to bury her femininity under a quiet, but self-assertive efficiency, which she thought a man would affect. Hungry and penniless though he was, Maurice could not help but notice how physically attractive this willowy woman with darkly coiled hair was as she strode across the reception of 'Yacht Owner' magazine in the Strand.

He was there to find a frontispiece for his book 'Yachting On A Small Income'. Already he had provided the journal with articles for which he had not been paid. Now he hoped at least to reap some benefit from their photo library. After making his request they had sent him down to Dulcie Kennard, who had recently been elevated from sub-editor and proof-reader on the magazine to acting editor.

Peter Gerard

Unbeknown to either of them it was a stop gap move while new management pared the staff to the bone, rearranged finances and cut editorial investment in a bid to save the doomed organ.

Dulcie, who, in her 'man's world', wrote under the name Peter Gerard, and who quickly became referred to by one and all as 'Peter', had also noticed Maurice.

Years later she described him thus: "... with a square jaw, good looks and little more than he stood up in."

As part of the new editorial economies the

magazine's freshly appointed 'whizz kid' decided to reject one of Maurice's articles.

"Now I don't think that's much of an article, people don't want to be told that sort of twaddle in a journal of this sort; it's babyish; like teaching a man how to brush his teeth," was how he broke the news to his acting editor.

Peter, not only impressed by the depth of Maurice's knowledge, but now attracted by the sailor with the goatee beard that looked irresistibly Elizabethan, became undiplomatically rash in her defence of her contributor.

Having ascertained that her boss had no yachting experience himself, she chimed: "Then I don't see quite how you are in a position to know what yachtsmen want to read about ... I myself am not an expert, but I know a bit about small yachts and I for one learnt a lot by that article."

The offending article was returned to Maurice with a full explanation from Peter as to what had happened. He sent in an alternative with a cover note expressing clearly his views on the manager and his opinion. Disastrously, Peter forgot to remove the cover note when the article was sent on to the printers.

"Later of course, the recipient was subjected to the unusual experience of seeing himself as others saw him, and in the fullness of time, which naturally developed rapidly, our further services were dispensed with after being accused of dark conspiracies," Peter recalls.

Like a pair of Bisto orphans, Peter and Maurice, or 'Bungo' as she called him, trudged the streets of London from Richmond to Gravesend looking at boats. Using Dutch finances they bussed around learning about each other. Maurice discovered Peter was a year older than he, the daughter of a cavalry colonel and that she had been introduced to yachting via hired sailing dinghies, which she helmed precariously in and around Lyme Bay.

She reminded Maurice of Lena's heroines. Here was a very independent woman, with strong views, who did a 'man's job'.

"I've always had a slight leaning towards the emancipation of women - an admiration for women who do things well and don't merely ape men," Maurice said later.

Both faced the uncertainties of freelance writing. Of Maurice, Peter recalled: "Bungo made ends meet by hard work, tireless canvassing of his mental products and occasional commissions for the sale and survey of small craft, a useful remnant of bygone days when he had managed to work up a small independent brokerage in his home river town up north."

At one stage Maurice shipped aboard a motorcruiser for a passage to France. He was paid for his knowledge of marine engines, a subject he had beefed up on since having his own aboard *Storm*. Maurice also hoped to write his articles from France - a cheaper country to exist in, then and now.

But he soon returned "... for economic and, I learnt later, sentimental reasons," Peter wrote.

Maurice, after many lonely months in his bedsit, had found what seemed the ideal partner - an attractive female who liked boats. Consequently he decided to try to find another cheap yacht that they could share, to counterbalance the gloomy grind of earning a living. The train timetable was consulted again and the pair set off to search in territory fresh to Peter, but well known to Maurice.

At Burnham-on-Crouch during their third weekend's hunting they came across *Puffin II* squatting in a mudberth. The 6 ton, 31-footer, built in Bideford in 1897, and resembling the great West Country schooners constructed in

Puffin II *at Burnham*

that port, had a draught creeping back towards that of *Undine* - 4ft 8in - but her clipper bow reminded Peter of the *Cutty Sark* and Maurice, ever preoccupied with the next article, conceded that, at least, she was of a type he had not experienced before.

Ipswich held too many recent sore memories for Maurice and a mooring on the Orwell was dismissed. Pin Mill was also too far a location to get to by train for a London-based freelance. Maldon, in Essex, and the nearby half tide moorings off Heybridge Basin, was his next yachting base. He sailed *Puffin II* round from Burnham one night through the Rays'n Channel on a falling tide.

Shocked by her rocking horse characteristic of pitching, he was even more concerned when the deep-keeler grounded on the Buxey.

"*Puffin* descended from the back of a sea with a grinding thump, lifted her counter, rode ahead on another sea, dropped slowly and thumped again, heavily. The next sea smashed against her counter in a smother of foam, and the dinghy rode past us on its crest until the little boat was somewhere under our lee bow."

With sheets hardened in, *Puffin II* ground her way across the hard sand, her boom end missing the "signpost at the crossways" of the Buxey beacon by inches and fortunately drove into deeper water once more.

Pretty though she was, *Puffin II* was not blessed with the kind of cabin Maurice had come to cherish. "Below decks *Puffin*'s accommodation was cramped and awkward. It seemed full of corners and senseless projections. The berths were almost too narrow to sleep on, yet the floor space was scarcely enough for one's feet, and the edge of the carlings caught one in the back when sitting down. The headroom was low because the foolish builders had made the cabin top almost flat, when, with fair camber, which would have also strengthened the beams, another seven or eight inches could easily have been obtained."

It was while Maurice owned *Puffin II* that he got his job with 'Yacht Sales And Charters'. As a result Peter had more time to enjoy sailing the boat than he. Peter had romantic ideas about the sea. She read all the deep sea voyage accounts - indeed she had reviewed the clipper authors, such as Basil Lubbock, for the yachting press. During her early sailing on the South Coast she imagined herself to be in the wake of the tea clippers racing home up Channel.

So her first experience on the East Coast came as a rude shock.

Singlehanded, she set off for the first time aboard *Puffin II* down the Blackwater from the couple's Heybridge mooring.

"Two islands there were to be negotiated; Northey and Osea; and the river being shallow in unexpected places leaves only a slim, navigable channel round one side of each at low water ...

"From where I started, the first island takes its character so much from the mainland that it might easily be overlooked as an island by one not knowing the river, unless a bird's eye view were possible of the muddy creek separating it from the farther side."

As a result Peter mistook Northey for the mainland and Osea for Northey, thus sailing north of the latter.

"Suddenly, glancing over the side, I was shocked to see the bottom going by quite clearly and had no idea which way to turn to regain deep water."

Puffin II

No matter which way she looked, the patchy green and brown bottom rose up to meet her. One minute she would seem to pull clear into a pool and the next would be tripping up on some obstruction like a well stuffed bolster. Several long minutes of shattering doubt ended abruptly as *Puffin* stopped dead.

"Hummocks of soft mud were appearing everywhere for over a mile round. The ebb rushed and swirled past *Puffin*'s prostrate form, and it seemed no time before she was lying over on her side at an acute angle, followed by her dinghy which at least sat upright beside her.

"On every hand the shiny sucking clay stretched away in

uneven heights and hollows like desert sand dunes; green weed sprawled over it in dead slimy patches and soft shelled crabs sidled aimlessly about like deserted brainless idiots."

To Peter's dismay she realised the tides were beginning to take off - that she had grounded *Puffin II* on The Stumble shortly after high water and that if she didn't manage to get her off on the next tide she faced being stranded there for a fortnight!

A kindly fellow yachtsman had spotted the little clipper high up on the mud and that night helped Peter kedge her off.

From there Peter had decided to get out of the muddy little river and into some real sea for a passage round to Burnham, but having read the chart, she concluded her first observations of the East Coast with the following:

"The chart showed me an intricate network of channels broken up by extensive spits and banks, which reminded me forcibly of The Stumble, with the added awe that these were not in a river but off the coast proper, thickly infesting the unprotected waters of the Thames Estuary covering some 40 miles north to south and 30 miles to the eastward. Had I been dropped into the middle of the Greek Archipelago I could not have navigated those hidden sands with more apprehension, unwilling to trust my own chart readings for two minutes together, but I must look again, measure up mileage, and take another sounding."

Peter had arrived in the swatchways.

10

The Editor's Chair

At Maldon

I n the 1920s yacht clubs did not have car parks. They did not need them. The boating fraternity travelled to their craft all over south and east England by train. Charles Pears even produced a book - 'Yachting on the Sunshine Coast' - which was published by the Southern Railway Company and gave train times to all the harbours mentioned.

This of course delighted Maurice. The two loves of his life could be indulged in one activity.

The railway companies offered special fares to yachtsmen to fill up their commuter trains at weekends. The London and North Eastern Railway created a weekend return for a single fare plus one third and it was a generous weekend - from midday on Friday until midday on the Monday. Not only that but the 'yachtsman's weekend ticket' allowed the holder to use the return to come back from a different destination from the one booked. If the secondary port was further from Liverpool Street station than the outgoing one then a nominal excess mileage was charged.

General stores at the tiniest ports from Queenborough to Aldeburgh stayed open late on a Friday night so that yachtsmen could stock up on perishables.

Maurice and Peter, their rail returns stowed in a hip pocket, humped backpacks off the train every Friday and, if *Puffin II* was at her Heybridge mooring, would walk from the

Peter in her flannels

station at Maldon stopping only to purchase "Bread, sausages, meat, bacon, eggs, tinned milk ..."

More often than not it was Peter making the train journey alone as Maurice, grateful for the real start he'd got in London, put his all into 'Yacht Sales and Charters'.

The sinewy, tough and, in her own words, "youthful piece of string that will stand a good deal of wear in the cause of little ships", daughter of a Dragoon Guard, was young enough to carry the unusual garb of grey flannel trousers and grey crew neck jumper without looking eccentric. Such wear for women was unheard of then, but Peter was a feminist before they'd been invented.

At six o'clock one morning in Bradwell, Peter came ashore with a letter to post to Maurice. Never mind the time of day, Peter wanted a stamp. The fact that the local store and the pub were closed mattered not to her - she had a tide to catch. Throwing gravel at the upper storey window of a house she got a response from the maid.

This is what she saw:

"To a person so lately asleep my appearance must have been something of a startler for the moment, with rough grey trousers bagging over the tops of sea-boots like a buccaneer, surmounted by an old fisherman's jersey, reefer jacket and

sou'wester whose ear flaps quite concealed my cropped
female head. However, as soon as she became assured from
my voice and features that I was not a hermaphrodite brig but
a pure bred sister under my outers, she became intelligent,
supplied my wants and went back to bed ..."

Here was a girl who, singlehanded, could haul up 40 lb of
anchor and 21 fathoms of ⅜in chain, without a winch. It once
took her an hour to haul in 90 ft of *Puffin II*'s cable.

"She was naturally physically strong. She was very wiry
and tough - a fairly slight and slender girl, but very tough
indeed," Maurice recalls today.

Another time, while getting *Puffin II* under way
singlehanded in the Crouch, she failed to get the mainsail on
her quickly enough. Sluggishly the little clipper fell away and
sailed hard on to the mud. As she did so Peter ran forward
and let go the anchor. The chain jumped out of the fairlead,
skinning two of Peter's fingers to the bone, before sawing
through several lays of the boat's shroud lanyards.

"The sails were stained in great streaks and patches where
I had touched them and the foredeck was an appalling sight
with every evidence that a murder had been committed. I felt
convinced that the skin had been shorn off both hands."

Having dipped her hands in stinging seawater, swabbed
down the blood and reeved off fresh lanyards, Peter tried
again and successfully left the Crouch the following day.

Bound for Brightlingsea she steered nervously through the
Rays'n leaving the Buxey beacon safely behind.

"I glanced astern. There in the metallic sunlight the magic
hills were beginning to show, their saffron backs curved
above the water level, stretching greedy tongues and fingers
into the path I had just vacated."

With a sense of triumph over the estuarine mud Peter
conjured up her destination.

"Meanwhile 'Brittlesea' (as the locals call it) had a cinema;
the Oyster Police would welcome me as always on their beat
up and down the river; and with luck I might intercept an in-
coming smacksman on his way to deliver his catch of fresh
cooked shrimps to a London train.

"I thought how well it would sound to say I'd left the
Roach before lunch and attended the pictures at Brightlingsea
for the evening performance. I wondered whether I ought to
change into a skirt for that, but recollecting that it would be
mostly dark, decided that trousers would be safer for a girl by
herself. I can always pass as a boy in uncertain light."

Alas it was not to be - yet.

Puffin II ran aground on the shallow knobs that mark the Knoll sand. There would be no cinema tonight. There wouldn't even be a stroll on the granite hard sands - for they rarely uncover.

Peter turned in as daylight receded - she would get nearly five hours before *Puffin II* could be freed.

Unlike Maurice, Peter did not believe her ship was too deep. She was thinking her seas were not deep enough.

As *Puffin II* stirred once more: "Remembering her plight in a rush of foreboding I burst out of the cabin to be dazzled by a blinding white light, and then leaned against the boom with relief. It was only the moon which shone high, bright and clear of any rings now, picking out everything in black and silver, while the new flood crept rapidly about the hull."

Maurice was not impressed with *Puffin II*'s draught. "Several times I had to spend eight uncomfortable hours crawling about her cramped cabin at an angle of 45 degrees,

A seasonal cover

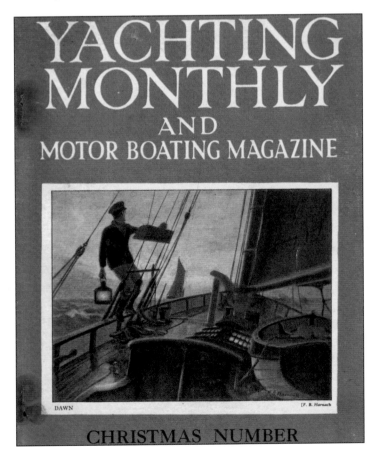

YACHTING
MONTHLY
AND
MOTOR BOATING MAGAZINE

DAWN   [F. B. Hornach]

CHRISTMAS NUMBER

through arriving too late for the tide."

On one occasion he and a shipmate had gone ashore just below *Puffin II*'s mooring at Heybridge on a falling tide. Maurice ordered his crew up on one sidedeck while he stood on the other in an attempt to get the boat to settle upright in the ooze. They succeeded and went below, resigned to a long wait, but at least a comfortable supper. While tucking into kippers, buttered bread and hot tea, *Puffin II* changed her mind and flopped over to starboard, dumping the hot tea and kippers in Maurice's lap.

There was nothing he could do about her keel and instead concentrated on her cabin. He wanted to alter *Puffin II* to make her a more suitable cruising boat. He had plans to raise the cabin roof, fit foldaway bunks, make more locker space and re-design the galley.

It was all too much. He was only getting aboard twice a month at most - his editorship of 'Yacht Sales and Charters' claimed most of his time and energy. Indeed he had made the paper a success. So much so that the parent magazine - 'Yachting Monthly' - was losing a small fortune in advertising revenue. The trouble was that all the main brokers resented the competition that 'Yacht Sales and Charters' gave them. Here was a magazine that advertised its own wares - it was outrageous!

"It was not foreseen that this ingenious scheme would put the backs up of all the established yacht brokers who not only refused, naturally enough, to buy space in its pages, but because the paper was related to the 'Yachting Monthly' stopped advertising in the parent magazine as well," Maurice reflects.

'Yachting Monthly' had then been in existence for 20 years. It was founded by one Herbert Reiach who had been on the staff of 'The Field'. He was a keen sailing man who had studied naval architecture and also painted marine pictures. When he died in 1921, aboard his boat, the editorship of 'Yachting Monthly' was taken by Malden Heckstall-Smith, known as 'Bookstall-Smith' in the trade, who was "completely wrapped up" in the social side of yachting.

This did not suit YM readers at all.

"He ruined, he really ruined 'Yachting Monthly' for five years from 1921 - 1926," Maurice comments vehemently as he looks back.

When the decision came to kill off 'Yacht Sales and Charters' by amalgamating it with YM, Maurice was asked to do the job and take over as Editor of the result. His first edition as Editor was that of January 1927.

As Peter Spectre, Assistant Editor of the US magazine 'Wooden Boat' observed over 60 years later, Maurice was a puzzling option.

"By contemporary standards - you must remember that this was England between the wars, when connections were the most important thing a young man could have - Maurice Griffiths was an odd choice."

The American went on to support his conclusion:

"His formal education had ended when he was 16, he did not have a university degree, he had worked in a real estate agency and he was living in a rooming house in London. His best connections were, perhaps, the lock keeper at the basin in Heybridge or the managers of backwater boatyards in Essex and Suffolk. He didn't know much about the Royal Yacht Squadron and what's more didn't seem to care. His best recommendations were his ability to kedge a small boat off a mudflat and use a sweep in the absence of a breeze to manoeuvre up the River Orwell with the tide ..."

In complete contrast to the supplicant panderings his predecessor had made to the South Coast brigade - their paid hands, their handicapped match racing, their fashion wear, their society fixtures and who among them managed to get aboard the royal yacht during Cowes Week - Maurice was soon in his stride, publishing a series of articles entitled 'Lifeboat into Yacht'!

Maurice had realised there was an unlimited source of hulls to be had from Bitterne near Southampton at a yard where thousands of wooden lifeboats were stored. Insurance underwriters insisted that these boats, especially those on ships whose passage took them through the Tropics, had to be replaced every five years. This of course applied whether they had gone rotten or not. Consequently there were hundreds of sound wooden hulls just waiting to be converted into yachts. They ranged in size from 21ft to 40ft and could be bought for as little as £30.

"Mind you, you had to do a lot of work - you had to take the thwarts out and the hoisting gear and so on, but you had a hull," says Maurice. "Yachtsmen and fishermen converted these lifeboats right up until the war. It wasn't until they were made of aluminium or steel that the supply dried up.

"It was almost a hidden source of boating. You'd find them all over the place, riz-ons and tore-outs they were known as."

Yet they could make excellent little yachts if converted properly.

There was also no shortage of enthusiasts. The YM articles proved so popular that the editorial staff were obliged to bring out the series in a collective leaflet, which sold at two and six (12½ pence) a time on the old faithful outlet - railway booth bookstalls. Before the run of these ended, 17,000 had been sold.

"It was astonishing. We carried rather nice photos of the successful ones, with different rigs, different layout plans, different engines. Many people just bought it to read on the train," remembers Maurice.

As Mr Spectre commented: "Maurice Griffiths did more to democratise yachting and boating in Great Britain than anyone else ..."

To compensate for his increased hours in London, Maurice, inspired by a reader's letter, was one of a dozen yachtsmen who founded the Little Ship Club in the winter of 1926. The idea was for lovers of the sea and ships, who were hide bound in the capital, at least to be able to talk about their interest. The early meetings were held at the Ship Tavern in Whitehall.

11

Wedlock

The imposing church of St Clement Danes in the Strand reminded Peter of a ship, surrounded as it was, and is, by a sea, albeit of tarmac. On approaching the Reverend Pennington-Bickford she discovered that his rectory was called 'The Anchorage'. What better place could there be for her wedding to Maurice Griffiths?

The couple had decided on a floating home and as *Puffin II* was clearly unsuitable she was sold. It was on the Crouch again that they found a boat that could accommodate them both comfortably. *Afrin* was a 34ft ex-Lowestoft pilot boat. The 10 ton gaff cutter was built in 1883 and had a draught of 4ft 2in.

Afrin

She had a wide fo'c'sle complete with galley and pipecot bunks, a self-contained loo, and a 10ft by 9ft saloon lined out with teak panelling. There was a two cylinder Kelvin which provided much needed back up in light airs. The boat had been converted to a yacht by an Ipswich house builder and consequently she was as near a floating home as the couple could wish for.

Just before the wedding *Afrin* was moored at Bradwell - miles from any convenient railway station - and it was Peter's task, while Maurice organised an office delegate to cover for him while he was away on honeymoon, to victual the ship. She sailed their

"We sailed Afrin hard up and down the coast"

dinghy from Bradwell to Heybridge for a crate of stores. On the return trip a stiff easterly dismasted the dinghy, called *Wild Oat* for its tendency to go on the loose while being towed, and Peter rowed the last two miles to *Afrin*.

The next day was the wedding day! As Peter laconically noted: "... according to all accepted standards, I might have been expected to have been more concerned with my trousseau and final hours of pristine purity."

The honeymoon was planned - Mr and Mrs Griffiths would sail to Holland.

Unfortunately, the early summer easterlies had set in, pinning the heavy old boat to the East Coast. Both were very fed up with her unhandiness; she carried dreadful weather helm even in such light weather. As they reached between the Ore and the Blackwater, Peter began to curse their new ship.

"You're nothing but a hard-mouthed old cow!" Peter cursed as she helmed, bitterly disappointed with the boat's performance.

While turning down the River Crouch Afrin's sluggardliness in stays almost put her athwart a moored yacht.

"She's a bitch!" yelled Peter as Maurice quietly grimaced to himself.

Peter's recollection of the honeymoon heartache was perceptive: "She made us swear so much we often didn't know whether we were swearing at her or being unkind to each other."

What should have been a 'yachtsman's happiest memory' turned out to be another valuable lesson, as *Afrin* blundered on to a mud spit below Waldringfield on the Deben and sat there for five hours. Maurice spent the time re-stowing almost half a ton of rusty fire bar ballast from the forepeak to the cabin well. When *Afrin* refloated they had a different boat altogether.

"We've tamed her," Peter said, her black mood turning sunny once more as she clasped the 6ft teak, rope-carved tiller of a beautifully balanced *Afrin*.

"Peter's weatherbeaten face wore a kindlier expression," Maurice recalled later.

The 10-day honeymoon was coming to a close and the newlyweds needed to find a berth for *Afrin* from which Maurice could get a train to London and the offices of 'Yachting Monthly'.

They returned to the place that had first captivated him with its peace - the Walton Backwaters. A good anchorage was found off the junction of The Twizzle and Foundry Reach and there *Afrin* swung round her anchor while Maurice caught the eight o'clock train from Walton station to Liverpool Street, returning to the boat on the 5.30pm train five days a week.

"There was a tea car on the 5.30 down and that helped one and of course the journey did give one time to read proofs or write, but it was cruel commuting - an hour and three quarters each way," Maurice remembers.

Walton itself was a 30 minute row in the dinghy or 15 minutes with a fair wind. At low water it was a hike across fields, dykes and stiles. Often, after rain, Peter would meet Maurice at the station with his oilskins and seaboots. After heavy rain during the night the pair would frantically bail out the dinghy before setting off, which made them late and, Peter wrote, "I would row while Bungo finished a final slice of bread and marmalade."

If *Afrin* was wind-rode out of the channel and up on the mud then 'Ooatie', as Peter affectionately called the dinghy, was used alternately to toboggan down the bank or with grapnel anchor and oars as ski sticks to haul her up.

Peter knew all this extra labour for a working commuter was no picnic, but felt her lot was no bowl of cherries either. "My own existence as wife, cook, caterer, freelance journalist, boatswain, valet and shipwright, could hardly be called idle ..."

"I seldom went up to town, lived in trousers, sweaters and sandshoes and reclaimed some unlived chapters of early youth by running more or less wild."

Through his growing number of contacts at YM, Maurice received an invitation to sail in the Fastnet Race that year from Conor O'Brien, who had sailed his brigantine *Saoirse* around the world and told those interested all about it in his book 'Across Three Oceans'.

Conor was to ship his sister, Kate, as crew and thought Maurice and Peter would help complement a happy and balanced team. Peter was very excited at the thought of sailing in a squarerigger in 'real' deep water.

The night before the race Peter was furious when she and Kate were turned away from the pre-race dinner at the Island Sailing Club in Cowes.

"Arriving at the doors of the club at the appointed hour with Conor, the officers were quite unable gracefully to swallow their surprise at the presence among the crews, of two women; and through a very transparent veil of courtesy pleaded, after a feverish consultation in the passage beyond, that there was no room for us ...

"Such treatment was difficult to forget in that post-war era of revised values, and contributed largely to a certain bitterness and contempt I felt thereafter for the average yacht club as an institution. Especially as on a later, similar occasion on the East Coast at the start of a Whitsun rally (the second of a regular event), I found myself, although in command of my own vessel, herded into a club annex with a 'yachtsman's harem', there to be regaled with nothing more exciting than plates of sandwiches and soft drinks!"

Of the affair Maurice said, "I think Kate took it more calmly than Peter - she'd stamp out of anything like that ... she'd storm out of a place and fight it."

A fresh sou'wester was blowing next morning as the 20 ton, 42-footer nosed out in the misty rain of Spithead and it was not long before *Saoirse*'s crew started reducing sail. Soon

(Left)
Conor
O'Brien's good
ship up for a
scrub before the
race

(Right)
Saoirse's crew,
from left back to
right front: Mr
Gibbon, Miss
O'Brien,
Mr Byford,
Captain
Holberton,
Maurice
Griffiths, Capt.
Conor O'Brien,
and "Con",
paid hand

Peter was finding out just how disheartening it was to sail a squarerigger to windward. Peter was first to succumb to seasickness and as darkness came on that first evening, the sight of the Guernsey mail steamer "plunging her bows into the troughs until her propellers raced in the air" did nothing to help the thought of the night ahead.

Peter was so ill she had to drop out of her watch and lay exhausted in the fo'c'sle for 27 hours until:

"Someone touched me on the shoulder. It was Bungo, black and shining in his oilskins, the water dripping dismally from them on to the bare boards of the fo'c'sle.

"Your wheel, Pete: come on old thing, you'll feel better if you can get on deck ... I've just managed to eat something," said Maurice.

Maurice had been up on the yard stowing the square topsail with Conor when the ship took a violent sheer upwind almost throwing them off.

"Buck up," Maurice continued. "Kate will be down in a minute ... and I don't mind telling you she nearly had us off that damned yard just now while we were reefing: and she's frightened to death of Conor which doesn't help matters."

By now it was blowing a full gale. Of the 15 starters, 13 had retired including *Saoirse* - Conor had ordered her to run back while off Portland Bill after a wave filled his chartroom. The distance covered in two days to windward was covered in

10 hours downwind. For six of those Peter was at the helm. She was pleased to be able to make up for her lost watches and flattered that Conor thought her the best helmsman aboard and the best hand he'd ever had.

With her oilskin pockets full of biscuits Peter revelled in the glorious sail back to the Solent:

"If you can imagine steep downland country like Cumberland suddenly come to life beneath you crowding upon you, pursuing you as you try to run away, catching you up, passing you: if instead of acres of green scrub and rounded hills, their summits ridged and glittered a rich emerald green transparent in the sun, and breaking into boiling foam that spreads sheets of lace work on a ground of black marble for miles around, you will have some idea of a high following sea in a full gale."

The first seven months of married life had been put to a severe test living aboard *Afrin*. Their many friends could not come and stay as the spare berths were filled with suitcases and if Maurice had to stay in town on business, Peter could not set sail on her own as *Afrin* was too much to handle alone.

That November of 1927 they both left *Afrin* to herself and rented a flat in London's Hampstead. The following month, tired of the metropolis, they returned to *Afrin* on Christmas Eve champing at the bit for a sail.

Peter was dressed in three jerseys, a reefer jacket, thick trousers tucked into thigh boots and over all a muffler, an oilskin and a wool cap. Yet still the perishing air of the Backwaters made her shiver.

"Pull away, old man, it's getting horribly cold out here!" she said as Maurice rowed the dinghy away from the Walton & Frinton Yacht Club.

Once aboard Peter stowed away a bumper locker load of Christmas food while Maurice got the coal stove going. The cabin thermometer rose steadily from 40 degrees to 68 deg F.

As Maurice sat in the cockpit watching the stars of a sharp, clear night, Peter prepared a roast dinner. The beckoning lights of Dovercourt twinkled an invitation for a night sail ...

"An hour later *Afrin*'s heavy mainsail went up, and with her jib and staysail drawing she rustled down the lonely creek, while the smoke from the chimney floated past the ray of light from the cabin port-holes like an endless procession of phantom forms.

"... I sat without a coat on the foredeck, which was dry from the warmth below, and when my hands got cold I warmed them round the chimney. We slipped past an anchored barge, silent and eerie in the rays from her riding light."

Maurice's trance was broken by Peter who was helming: "Mainsheet," she barked and her husband eased out the boom as they ran into the Stour.

Afrin sailed on into a "world of gloom and eternal night", but beneath the stove-dry decks "we had our own little world with us".

They anchored below the bluff cliff at Wrabness and descended below into the cosy cabin. *Afrin* lay silently on a black river. Only the curling smoke from her chimney would have told a late passer-by on the beach that she was inhabited.

Below, Maurice tapped the barometer.

"The glass is extraordinarily high and still rising," he said.

"Wind. From the east," came Peter's uncompromising reply.

"But it's a bally flat calm!"

Using one of the weather maps Peter received every morning from the Met Office, she instructed the city-bound yachtsman.

"There's an area of unusually high pressure centred here, and it's moved that much since yesterday. If we don't get a pretty fresh easterly wind tomorrow ...""... You'll become a nun, movie star, or police woman, and give up yachting and me. Well, we're all ready to clear out if need be," said Maurice, his jest deflating the rather unnecessarily grave delivery of his new wife.

However, she was right. Next day as they sailed *Afrin* round to Pin Mill for Christmas Day a blizzard raged round them courtesy of half a gale of wind from the northeast.

Sailing in such bitter weather when most yachts were high and dry for the winter helped Peter identify with the hard-bitten seamen she had read about in the Basil Lubbock books she reviewed for the yachting press.

She struck a challenging pose which Maurice noticed.

"I have a vivid recollection of the shipmate standing on the slanting weather deck like a young smacksman, her red thigh boots wide apart, a muffler and blue stocking cap almost meeting at her nose, her right hand thrust into her jacket pocket, the other holding the tiller line ..."

12

Down Channel

The indomitable Peter Gerard felt there was a lack of equality in the sailing partnership with her husband. Maurice had spent all those bachelor days in his many boats as a man alone. Why should she not have the same opportunity to discover her abilities for herself? Peter ignored the fact that she had probably enjoyed a finer grounding in boat handling than her spouse - Maurice had never sailed dinghies.

"I shall never rest until I have my very own ship," she announced.

Maurice was a little hurt by this statement, but was beginning to learn that it was useless trying to fight against his wife's headstrong plans.

"... with a sinking feeling that I could not express, I knew that it was true."

So *Afrin* was sold and not long after sank on the Cutler bank off Bawdsey - her garboards torn out on the ragged remains of the wreck of HMS *Arethusa*.

Peter later wrote: "I had always hankered for the absorbing interest of a little vessel I could call my own and on which I could try out ideas and experiments without going into conference..."

When mutual friends protested at the idea of the apparently perfect yachting couple having separate boats Peter was unsympathetic.

"No one is surprised if a modern wife flies her own light aeroplane, rides her own horse, or has a separate car; yet because a boat with a lid on it at once acquires some of the characteristics of a shore residence they regard it with the same concern that might be shown on learning that a happily married pair lived in separate flats!"

Peter admitted that her own dogmatic approach to "shipology" was a "pain in the neck" to Maurice who, unlike his wife, was not bewitched by the nomenclature of matters maritime, but rather was more interested in the practicalities of boats underway.

Ships to 'Bungo' were, Peter observed, "not almost human entities as they are to me; and once his existing 'slave girl' had made him familiar with all her vices and virtues, the sultan became restless for new conquests."

With her share of *Afrin*'s proceeds she bought *Juanita*, a 32ft West Country yawl, with standing headroom and a 6ft draught - totally unsuitable, in Maurice's opinion, for the East Coast.

Adept at turning the world of sexual chauvinism upside down, Peter had produced the yachting world's first 'boat widower'!

A rueful Maurice lamented: "Although it was patent that my partner adored this long-legged craft and spent weeks, from dawn till darkness, working on her, scraping, varnishing, painting, and improving the accommodation below decks, I hoped inwardly that in due course, in two, maybe three, years, she would tire of her independent ownership, and be willing to share my own craft once more. It would, I felt, be worth waiting for ..."

Unlike her marriage, as it turned out, only death parted Peter from Juanita.

Home for the Griffiths became a First World War ML, the 80ft *Night Mist*, which they moored in a mud puddle at Walton itself. "She was in a fairly ropy condition," Maurice later recalled.

With his wife chasing off down Channel in search of real waves and tall ship weather in her deep sea yacht, Maurice was obliged to buy his own seagoing boat if he wanted to enjoy the fruits of marriage.

As a result he went completely against all the conclusions he had drawn from his considerable experience of yachts and yachting and bought the deepest boat he would ever own.

Wilful had once belonged to George Muhlhauser, the First World War Royal Naval Reserve Lieutenant who later made a circumnavigation in the 37 ton yawl *Amaryllis*. The heavy, beamy old gaff cutter therefore had a pedigree that Peter approved of. She was built by Sibbick of Cowes in 1899. The eight-tonner was 30ft to the stemhead, with an eight and a half foot beam and drew a swatch-busting 5ft 6in. She had a dark mahogany panelled cabin and a brass fireplace with a tiled surround. A small separate ladies cabin had been turned into an engine room for the Kelvin auxiliary.

Now there were two deep draught yachts moored in The Twizzle and both of them regularly tripped over the Pye

Sand on their way to and from the Backwaters.

No longer would Messum's East Coast Rivers pilot be sufficient guide aboard *Wilful* and Maurice spent lunchtimes out of his office poring over charts of the Channel in Captain O M Watts' shop in the West End. In that summer of 1928 he bought charts to cover a passage down Channel and round into the Bay of Biscay as far as Belle Isle.

With his deep sea yacht and the promise of a blue water passage outside the parameters of the Thames Estuary, Maurice wooed Peter back aboard and she left *Juanita* swinging round her mooring for their summer holiday passage.

"Bungo approached his unusual role of deep-sea-dog with an open mind ... a true lover of sand-hills and swatchways only accessible to craft that will float on a heavy dew, he never affected a desire for the rigours of deep-water cruising which he did not genuinely feel, and would merely produce a tolerant little smile faintly tinged with pity when frisky pups like me bit his heels and barked, 'oh you ditch-crawler, come out and play on the main road!'" Peter recalled.

Maurice said: "Well, in *Wilful* I've certainly got a ship designed for the job; so we'll go my boy ... *Now* are you satisfied?"

Before they got round the North Foreland *Wilful*'s antifouling was worn off on an estuary shoal.

ML similar to the one which was MG and Peter's backwater home

"Suddenly we hit the bottom with that dreadful jarring thud that shakes all the rigging - lifted in the slight swell, glided noiselessly forward, descended gracefully, and - thud! Again and again. The gear was rattling and shaking and an odd cup in the pantry was clinking madly. Thud, thud! It was like hitting granite, and the jarring was so bad that it was difficult to keep our feet."

Maurice took some cross bearings which showed them to be where they should be in a swatchway, which according to the chart had two and a half fathoms through it. But *Wilful* had found the Knock John sand. She was lifting and dropping on "pavement-like sand, threatening to relieve herself of her 4½ ton lead keel."

With the sheets hard in and a shove from the engine they got her off and victualled the cockpit lockers with the biscuit barrel, fruit and water to refresh the helmsman throughout his and her night watches.

A fresh northeasterly pushed *Wilful* at speed through the Downs.

Underway the couple used the pet name 'Sonny' for whichever of them was not on the helm.

Using this affectionate nickname Maurice enthusiastically drew Peter's attention to the fair wind they had for a down Channel passage.

"We're not off the South Foreland yet," came her gloomy reply.

As night came on: "... three great seas, larger than all the others, roared up under our weather quarter, smothered the deck in foam and actually carried *Wilful* bodily to leeward as she nearly broached to with a sickening movement that was like leaping off a cliff." Peter did not want Maurice to take in a reef in case he was washed overboard, but *Wilful* was now over pressed so they hove to while Maurice wound down three rolls on the worm gear.

"What a run that was! A wild night in all truth, the roaring angry seas with their death-like blackness capped by a seething ghostly whiteness, the drenching, beating rain and the utter darkness that blotted out even our masthead."

Morning saw them off Dover and Maurice peered towards the great southwest from where the wind was now blowing.

"Down Channel the scene was just as I always seem to have known it - a grey tumbling waste of water and a cruel wind that blows up in one's teeth."

Peter was seasick, the glass was dropping, but Maurice ignored the beckoning arms of Dover's harbour walls as, once inside with a sou'wester blowing, "... you never leave, for the sight of white horses rolling past outside is sufficient to demoralise anyone."

So they beat on against the rising wind and for two days slammed back and forth across the Channel, making pitifully slow progress over the ground.

Peter recalled: "Conversation became as much a routine as the endless march of sunrise and sunset, the ebb and flow of tides, the cut-steel stars, the shifting clouds, and the bold deep blue of the Channel."

On the second night Maurice went off watch and turned in only to be awakened by a terrific crash. Leaping from his bunk he was appalled to see the wind had freshened further and that a limp Peter was steering from the leeward side of the cockpit. "It's easier to be sick this way," she explained.

Maurice took stock of the situation, reefed ship and decided they would give up their awful struggle, ease away the sheets and steer for Newhaven.

Peter lay in the cockpit well - too ill to face going into the stuffiness of the cabin. She dozed fitfully down beside Maurice's legs and out of the cold wind.

At six o'clock in the morning they sailed gratefully into the peaceful calm of Newhaven and moored alongside a Thames sailing barge also bound west, deep laden with cement.

The harbourmaster acquired a saint-like status when he announced: "My word, you must have had a night of it! You'll want to turn in for a few hours. I'll send someone to collect the dues at ten, not before."

For three days they rested up and in that time Maurice's mother, Lena, joined the ship for the proposed cruise on the 'Sunshine Coast'.

As the wind eased Maurice started to get *Wilful* ready for sea again. The wind was still in the southwest, which caused the barge skipper to advise Maurice to wait for a 'slant', but Maurice explained they had to get on and in any case *Wilful* was built for windward work.

To this the bargeman remarked that it didn't seem "fair" for the two "ladies" adding his unasked-for opinion that he didn't approve of women aboard ships anyway.

To his astonishment Peter said, "Go and boil your head."

On passage to the Solent they passed a steamer in the night and Maurice's description reminds one irresistibly of his earliest passion - the steam train.

"A door opened under her bridge and the figure of a man stood for an instant silhouetted against the orange rectangle.

Then it shut with a clang, and as we passed through the subdued medley of her wake a smell came down wind to us, a smell that is like none other on earth - the delicious haunting smell of a steamer, of coal and galley smoke, hot oil, steam and smoothly running engines ...”

Twenty-six hours out from Newhaven *Wilful* anchored in Wootton Creek and began two days of exploration in the Solent. They sailed to Beaulieu, Yarmouth and Cowes. With holiday time running short for Maurice they decided on the third night to head east again the following day and make the most of the sou'wester that had given them so much grief.

Alas the wind had now collapsed. *Wilful* took a day and a night to drift out as far as the Owers. Day two saw them drift and motor as far as Hastings, where they anchored for the night off the small stone fishing harbour.

At 4 am a Hastings lugger bashed alongside *Wilful* and as Maurice clambered wearily on deck her skipper threw some plaice and sole aboard - was he interested?

“I confess that at that moment, as I stared sleepily at the mess of slimy fish before me and the clumsy lugger ground her tarry side against *Wilful*'s white enamel, I cursed the Channel and everything in it from the depths of a tormented soul, and felt that if the elements would only let me get my ship back to the friendly old sands and swatchways, withies and creeks of the Thames Estuary, I would sell this 'deep-sea cruiser', even though she was the finest all-round small cruiser I have sailed aboard, and buy an old fisherman that would sit on the mud and give me peace - and a real holiday!”

Wilful motored on, ever eastwards, in the flat calm with Maurice cursing the engine's racket and hallucinating about swimming in a quiet creek in the hot sun.

Off Folkestone they ran out of paraffin fuel, but a passing 'sixpenny sick' tripper boat sold them five gallons worth and *Wilful* chugged into Dover harbour on the last day of Maurice's holiday.

Early next morning Maurice was on a train back to London and his office. Later in the day Lena left for home too. Peter was left in sole charge.

13

The First Design

Maurice kept a reasonable shore-going rig aboard *Wilful*, which was as well, for as the train pulled into Charing Cross station he hadn't time to go to the Hampstead flat and change.

'The Yachting Monthly', as the magazine was then rather grandly titled, had moved editorial office from King Street in Covent Garden to Clements Inn near the High Court. Maurice strode quickly along the Strand leaving the world of high sea frustration far behind him.

Shortly after Maurice's arrival at YM he was joined by the remarkably tall figure of Norman Clackson who had been brought in as the thrusting young executive hoping to gain overall control of advertising with his position as managing director.

Maurice was not one for boozy lunches; he was a self-confessed 'workaholic', but on rare occasions he and Norman would take sandwiches and a beer in a pub behind the office.

One day Maurice's brother Leslie came to meet him in London. They met in the same pub and when Norman came in he found a rather morose looking Maurice talking to a stranger.

"They didn't seem to be fond of each other at all. Maurice introduced me but didn't ask me to join them. They seemed dead quiet with each other and after a little while they cleared out. It was a very cold association, I thought, of two brothers," Norman recalls.

It may have been a cold association, but under the surface was a gentle compassion from Maurice towards his elder brother. Leslie had never been popular with his father, and on the rare outings sailing with Maurice had always been seasick. Yet the comparatively well off younger man paid for the private education of Leslie's second child, a boy, Bruce, at Highfield College in Leigh-on-Sea, Essex.

"Maurice was a damn good editor. He could write at the drop of a hat and lived off his pen. He wrote remarkable letters all about nothing but which were riveting," Norman recalls. "And we got on very well together because we kept ourselves to ourselves in our own departments. He wouldn't come along and tell me what to do and I wouldn't say I thought the content was a load of balls."

Norman found himself suffering from the legacy of 'Yacht Sales and Charters'. "When they packed it up I was left with the dirt - it had ruined any connection with getting any business from the brokers in London. And I had a hell of a time; if I hadn't been fairly tall [he is 6ft 5in] I would have been thrown out of offices. They were very rude but I don't mind people being rude because I am rude back to them."

From Maurice's very first days afloat he developed a critical eye for a boat's lines. "I like sometimes to sit in my dinghy and let the tide carry me through an anchorage on a still moonlit night; to drift silently past one yacht after another, watching their varied hulls slipping by in the half-light and musing on their qualities and character ..." He would have been far too polite to drift by in daylight.

Maurice was soon making sketches of hulls he had seen, and those he had not, on the backs of shopping lists and other scraps of paper. Features in YM on designs by T Harrison Butler, Luke, Payne, Albert Strange, Morgan Giles and others produced such enormous mail bags that Maurice decided to run design competitions and allow readers a platform for their own creations.

Maurice therefore had to make himself expert in boat design. He read all the literature he could on naval architecture and had already begun an association with Institution of Naval Architects member Frederick Shepherd in the days when YM's office was in King Street. The kindhearted designer's office was only a short walk away in Piccadilly and it was there Maurice spent many of his lunch hours. There in the drawing office Maurice learnt how to interpret hull form from lines, how to calculate weight over length and beam and how to draw curves without kinks. The years Maurice had spent buying and selling boats from East Coast yacht yards meant he had many contacts in the field. He was always welcome at these boat sheds and given free rein to wander about taking measurements, asking questions of the builders.

Through the pages of YM Maurice had regularly referred to the benefits of shoal draught yachts so it was not surprising when, in 1928, he received his first commission to build a wildfowling boat which could creep up the same creeks as the target fauna and sit like a duck on the low tide mud.

The client owned a big ketch which he moored on the Hamble. She drew 8ft and was therefore unsuitable to use for his winter pursuits shooting birds. Maurice designed *Wind Song* - she was not unlike his own *Wild Lone* to look at. The 28-footer drew 2ft 6in with centreplate and rudder plate hauled up. She had a cosy cabin with berths for two and a forepeak for the guns and Lurcher dog, warmed by the obligatory coal stove.

Wind Song, built of teak, was launched at Feltham's yard in Portsmouth in 1929.

"The benefits of shallow draught are obvious to sailors in this country now, but not then," Maurice comments today. "Yachtsmen couldn't understand that a boat with a centreboard, without a heavy deep keel, could still be safe at sea. This was in spite of the fact that American sailors would come over in centreboard boats and win races all over the place."

Wild Lone and *Swan* had their virtues, but Maurice was aware they could capsize and so he came to believe the best compromise was a centreboard and an outside ballast keel together to increase stability.

While sailing *Swan* Maurice had considered the possibility of having a boat with fixed 'leeboards' on the bottom and a central ballast keel. Unwittingly he had conceived the bilge keel. It was much later he realised that so too had Lord Riverdale who had launched a 24-footer, *Bluebird of Thorne*, with twin keels.

Next a birdwatcher from the wilds of Northumberland ordered a centreboarder that could dry out comfortably on moorings inside Holy Island. Maurice designed a gaff cutter with under 3ft draught on a 30ft length with a 9ft beam. *Loon* was built by Millers of St Monance in Fife and launched in 1930.

As well as their shallow bottoms both boats sported an MG original - a centreplate built in an L-shape, like a half opened pocket knife, with a hauling edge coming up through the foredeck. Maurice had invented such an arrangement to avoid having too much centreboard box taking up room in the cabin.

It was found, however, that when fully lowered the L-shaped plate had its leading edge ahead of the centre of effort of the sail plan. This made the boats luff up which was OK in light weather, but their owners had to rig tiller lines to counteract weather helm in fresh winds. Always ready to learn more, Maurice then began an in-depth research project into the centreboard.

"There wasn't much experience with centreboards in this country to draw on, so I did a lot of experimenting on paper trying to get the centres worked out.

"Most yachtsmen resisted shoal draught designs because they thought the boats were unstable, that they wouldn't be able to recover from a knock down. I always tried first off when designing a boat to produce a really seaworthy design. It shouldn't turn upside down and stay upside down. If it is knocked down it must come back. It is one of the essentials. You can make it as shallow as you like, but it must be stable enough to stay upright.

"I did my best to advocate what I considered to be sensible shoal draught boats. The readers seemed to take it very well. I would try to show through examples in the magazine how shallow draught boats came successfully through violent storms. 'Yachting Monthly' really got the thing going - developed much more interest. Boats didn't have to have deep, heavy keels in order to cross the Atlantic. But changing people's minds was a very slow process."

At the same time he was reading typescripts sent in by hopeful yachtsmen and vetting artwork from marine painters. Maurice began an association with some very fine artists. There was Edward Wigfull, an old-fashioned newspaper illustrator who wrote copy for the magazine as well under the pen name Handy Billy. His paintings invariably depicted yachts in very heavy weather, which was quite an imaginative feat living as he did on a houseboat in the sheltered waters of Benfleet Creek in Essex. Former Metropolitan Police Commissioner H Alker Tripp preferred muzzy etchings of fog or night passages. He too wrote for the YM under the byline Leigh Hoe. There was the inimitable Charles Pears ROI who painted from the deck of the yawl Maurice had sold him many years before.

However, of all the considerable talent supplying material for the growing circulation of YM, Fid Harnack's work became Maurice's favourite. Fid, a West Mersea man, loved the East Coast as much as his editor did and there was no one who could capture it like he. His great hobby was steamship spotting and with his brother Gus he produced a book, 'Ships and Shipping', full of thumbnail sketches of freighters passing in and out of the busy Thames Estuary deep water routes. Readers of YM would often find a passing steamship on the horizon of his artwork and Fid excelled in creating the yachtsman's worst nightmare - a close encounter with a big ship at sea.

One of Maurice's favourite YM covers was painted by Fid. It was the December 1933 issue. "I remember discussing with Fid how I wanted a laying up cover picture done. A good smack yacht or something similar with signs of somebody living aboard - with lights and a smokestack."

The result was one of the most evocative pictures of the East Coast ever to appear in YM.

Maurice's favourite cover

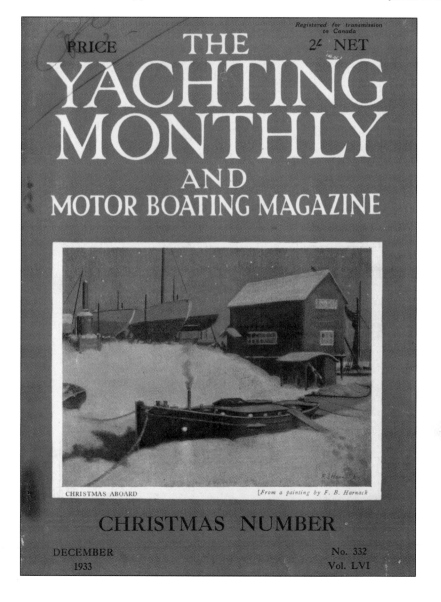

PRICE **THE** 2⁄ NET

Registered for transmission to Canada

YACHTING MONTHLY
AND
MOTOR BOATING MAGAZINE

CHRISTMAS ABOARD   [From a painting by F. B. Harnack

CHRISTMAS NUMBER

DECEMBER 1933   No. 332   Vol. LVI

14

Peter Is Rescued

Wilful lay rolling her guts out in the outer harbour at Dover. Peter walked round the town trying to purchase paraffin from various garages - it was early closing day and she was unable to buy the amount required at an ironmongers.

With the boat prepared for her passage back to The Twizzle, Peter set sail the following day intending to return the yacht in time for her rightful owner's forthcoming weekend.

A southerly breeze carried her quickly up through the Downs, past the North Foreland and then eased, leaving *Wilful* off the NE Spit with a foul tide for the Edinburgh Channel.

Wilful *at Bradwell – alongside a stack barge*

Peter, sailing singlehanded, fell into melancholia as the spars swung about uselessly. "The coast of Kent faded in a sea mist, the sun dropped towards a bank of oily cloud in the west. The loneliness was oppressive. An eerie menace seemed

hidden beneath those liquid hills that undulated about me like an endless tangle of caterpillars under a satin bedspread."

She was relieved when the engine started at the first attempt and steered *Wilful* ever northward, hour after hour, against the flood. After a few hours' steaming she made a nervous check of the engineroom, which revealed a sea of oil. As Peter could not discover where it was coming from she shut the Kelvin down. A fair wind returned and Peter continued on her course. She had hoped she was steering down the Black Deep, but hours after it should have shown, she still had not picked up the Sunk Sand Head.

Near dawn Peter thought she had picked up the Gunfleet Lighthouse, scene of her husband's near demise many years before, and soon she also made out some fishing luggers in the gloom. She steered down towards them hoping to get confirmation of the light.

When they answered in French she was completely thrown - surely she hadn't slid across the North Sea?

While attempting to make herself understood, one of the luggers collided with *Wilful,* splitting the rubbing strake and cracking the rail.

"After standing agape like a crowd of stuffed baboons, one of the crew, in response to my frantic appeals to fend off, jumped aboard me and assisted in getting me far enough from the blanketing lee of the lugger's high freeboard and sail to allow *Wilful*'s sail to draw again ..."

The fisherman leapt back aboard his own craft having told Peter she was, at least, not off the coast of France.

Wilful was close to the King's Channel, though whether she had crossed the middle part of the Sunk Sand or gone round the northern end, Peter wasn't really sure. Eventually, to the northwest, the Naze could be faintly seen, but a line squall approached. "The land darkened with shadow. It ran down the face of the cliffs swiftly as a jackal and spread out on the water beneath, a hard black line."

Quickly it set upon a motionless *Wilful* and blew out her mainsail. Peter started the Kelvin again without difficulty but it soon ran out of paraffin fuel.

Vainly Peter tried to tow the hefty old boat by rowing the dinghy with a line at right angles to her bow - if only she could get her head round and then anchor close in under the lee of a sand ...

But the windage on *Wilful* dragged Peter and the dinghy with her to leeward under bare pole.

Having quickly weighed up her predicament, Peter

realised her only hope of salvation lay with the luggers - now
downwind of her position. Desperately, she realised she
would have to row down to them - beating *Wilful* to it. It was
a calculated risk - they might heave up their nets and sail off
before she had got to them. In that case she would have
difficulty holding the dinghy up against wind and tide while
waiting for *Wilful* to drive down to her.

It was a risk she took and 20 minutes' stiff pulling had her
alongside the *Marcel Maurice of Gravelines.*

Her line was taken and Peter was heaved aboard the
lugger by a tough-looking crew.

"Deposited in their midst I felt like a rough-haired terrier
amongst a lot of mastiffs," she recalled.

"What do you want us to do?" asked the skipper.

"Pass a tow line and take my ship into Harwich," said
Peter.

"Where is that?" the skipper replied unfolding a very small
scale chart of the North Sea coasts.

Peter showed him.

"Much sand and little water there ... this boat is deep ... I
do not know," he said uncertainly.

"Yes, but I know: I will take you there: that is where we
must go," Peter demanded.

She won. Now her head was filled with doubts over
salvage claims and made the best attempt to strike up a
friendship during the five hours' steaming that lay ahead of
them. "I decided to build up an entente cordiale ... so that a
nice cake might come out of the oven by the time we got
there."

The fishermen yarned away, each trying to outdo the other
on the number of children they had. "They wanted to know if
I had any, and roared with laughter when I said ships were
my children."

The crew offered her extra clothing, biscuits and raw eggs
as Peter, in her role of pilot, steered the lugger, a fisherman
having been posted at the helm of the following *Wilful.*

She hoped that somehow this made her overall commander
of the flotilla, thereby weakening any subsequent salvage
liabilities.

At Harwich a helpful Lloyd's agent sorted out the payment
to be made to the fishing boat crew and they were happy
enough - even handing a large lobster over to Peter who had
been awake the 30 hours since leaving Dover.

The first Maurice knew of the rescue was in the Stop Press
of the 'London Evening News': "Yachtsman Lost in North

Sea."

On talking to Peter later she was furious that the paper had suggested she was lost.

"She said she knew where she was all the time," said Maurice. "I think she really was lost. She was out of sight of land."

Maurice believed it was only the curiosity of the fishermen that prevented them driving a harder salvage claim.

"I think they were so fascinated by this extraordinary creature, who was dressed like a man, who talked like a man, swore like a man and who could obviously handle a boat, because here she was all those miles off in a 30ft cutter, that they accepted something quite small."

Maurice blamed himself to some extent - the mainsail he admitted had been "fairly ripe", but he also partly blamed the sailmaker for he disapproved of the cloths running horizontal instead of parallel with the leech.

Commuting back and forth to London from *Night Mist* proved too much for Maurice and so their floating home was sold. Now Mr and Mrs Griffiths lived in the Hampstead flat commuting out at weekends to their respective boats.

The following year Maurice found his responsibilities at YM increasing and therefore offered *Wilful* out to a friend for three months' cruising in the West Country. Maurice would have a good sail though, getting her from the Backwaters to the Hamble where his pal would take over.

Once again Peter joined Maurice aboard *Wilful* and once again they set off down Channel. Again they were both seasick, again they faced a sou'west struggle. "I guessed we'd have plenty, with Cape Gris Nez looking so clear yesterday," said Peter sagely.

Dosing themselves with the patent medicine Mothersill and dipping into Ramsgate and Newhaven for respite against the foul Channel winds, they were not far short of the Solent when the jib outhaul carried away at night.

It was Maurice's boat so: "A new one must be rove, and the thought made me begin to feel very sick. For a time I debated whether to strip and endure the inevitable series of duckings in the icy wind, or whether to try and remain dry, like a deep-sea diver."

The thought of undressing below with the bowel-wrenching pitching of *Wilful*'s motion had Maurice lashed in oilskins and waders for the task. After a successful operation, during which Maurice was fully immersed several times in Channel seas, he was violently sick.

At last they pushed into the Hamble and there on the muddy side of the river lay his old boat *Puffin II*, a nostalgic reminder of the shelter and peace of the East Coast.

After *Wilful's* long cruise Maurice kept her on moorings at Warsash for the rest of the season. A lengthy train journey brought him down for the occasional weekend, but his mind was already made up.

"I have come to the conclusion that this 'seaworthiness at all costs' fetish is greatly overdone by owners and designers alike. Unless one deliberately courts disaster in Portland Race, or the North Sea in winter time, or off Ushant in a heavy westerly, a well-formed cruiser whose hull is essentially seakindly and does not break up the seas with too full waterlines, a spoon bow, or a long flat counter, seldom if ever, has 'solid water' dropped into her well, and, in my opinion, does not stand in dire need of a shallow, cramped, wet and chilly self-emptying cockpit."

Maurice never sailed *Wilful* back to the East Coast. She was sold where she belonged - in Channel waters.

That winter Maurice started making enquiries about the only boat he'd ever owned and not sold willingly.

Her owner, as it turned out, had jogged up and down the Deben for the last six years, depositing his family on suitable beaches for picnics. Now, for the summer of 1930, he felt he could do as well with a motor cruiser. *Storm* was on the market again.

Picture of Wilful, *taken by* Jack Coote

15

Shoal Draught

The search for the Holy Grail of hulls lead Maurice on a cerebral crossing of the Atlantic. It was the Americans who had the experience, the theories, the boats and the literature on shoal draught safety. In this field at least the US had left the 'greatest' seafaring nation on earth in the doldrums. Naturally conservative, traditionalist Britain was decades out of date with its obsessive 'seaworthiness equals depth' dogma. The Americans had ruled that out, had proved time and again with individual experience that well designed shoal draught boats were actually safer in a seaway.

Maurice began to discover this as he read through the yachting magazines of the US market. Basically a deep yacht stayed put in a seaway and, like a half tide rock, allowed waves to break over her. She relied on massively strong decks and exceptionally watertight openings to withstand the onslaught. A good shoal draught yacht, however, slid down the face and away from the oncoming, rising sea, the turbulence made by her hull even helping to break the wave before it reached her.

Charles II started yachting in Britain, on his return from exile in Holland, aboard a Dutch 'jacht'. Soon noblemen were having their own yachts built to race one another on the Thames. Speed being the most important consideration, it was hardly surprising the shipwrights copied the fastest boats of the day - the deep draught revenue cutters. Two hundred and fifty years later they were still building them like revenue cutters!

The generic names of late nineteenth century yachts gave them away: 'plank-on-edge' describing the frightening lack of beam, 'lead-mine' the depth and weight of keel to keep them upright, 'peg-top' depicted the slack-bilged, midsection.

"Tradition dictated that builders continue copying the revenue cutter style. There wasn't the call in this country for shallow-draught yachts, but there were many areas in Britain where there should have been, such as the Thames Estuary,

"Too much of a fair wind!"

the Solent and the River Dee. There were parts of the country where the fishing boats were shallow - they had to be - but not the yachts. It was very curious," Maurice comments.

But then 'cruising' was not yet a popular pastime of the British. Apart from a few wealthy eccentrics like Lieutenant E Middleton in his *Kate,* and Richard Turrel McMullen in various craft, all those who went yachting went racing. With their paid crews and seasonal sailing in sheltered waters such as the Clyde and the Solent, did it matter that their boats "went up and down in the same hole", sailed with the lee rail half the beam under water or nose dived into moderate seas? It was only when passage making that 'seakindliness' was paramount.

It was also during a sea passage that perhaps the ultimate design of revenue cutter styled yacht was lost. *Oona* was built in 1886 - 46ft on deck, 8ft draught, with a snake-hipped 5ft 6in beam. On her maiden voyage from Southampton to the Clyde with owner, designer, skipper and two hands aboard, her hull was driven ashore in Malahide after leaving Dun Laoghaire. The 10 ton lead keel had gone and all hands were lost.

Later during Maurice's first year as Editor of YM, the school teacher yachtsman Ernie Sinclair lost his short and deep Falmouth quay punt *Joan* off Greenland after she became overwhelmed and had her mast carried away by moderate seas.

When an order came for a 45ft gaff ketch with a shoal draught, Maurice went back to the drawing board with his research swimming in his head. He had been impressed by an American design, the 52ft ketch *Alice*, which had a draught of just 4ft with her centreboard raised. Her owner, Henry Howard, had described how, while riding out a gale, the seas "seemed as though they could not get hold of her".

Now his latest task, to provide a centreboarder for the Commodore of the Royal Egypt Yacht Club who wanted to explore shallow parts of the Nile, had also to have the seaworthy qualities required for cruising the Greek Islands.

The result was *Ionia*, built in Alexandria in 1933. She was 45ft 6in on deck, had a 13ft beam, and 4ft of draught with the wooden centreboard wound up. Maurice had been positively influenced by *Alice*.

Norman Clackson thought Maurice had been "bitten with this shoal draught stuff", but kept his thoughts to himself.

"He concentrated on his rivers and creeks, it's his type of country. He became the specialist on shallow draught boats in England anyway," Norman says now.

Away from the Channel and its seagoing yachts Maurice pottered happily about aboard *Storm* once more. He sailed her up to Woodbridge, there to have a Jack Tar coal stove fitted, an essential after using them in his intermediate yachts. Complete with a coal locker and a Woolworth's 'coal-glove' Maurice was ready for sea again!

It was early in March when Maurice and Peter sailed *Storm* back to her old mooring off Heybridge Basin. A

Juanita *and* Storm *in Heybridge Lock*

bitterly cold night passage had the pair taking short turns at the helm interspersed with coffee from an enamelled jug kept permanently on the stove and a loaf-load of buttered toast.

Once Peter came below while Maurice was pouring coffee and said, "Well, if she is a shallow old dish, thank heaven she can sail herself." But throughout the season as Maurice sat crook-backed under her low carlings, he began to wish *Storm* were just 5ft longer ...

One evening as he sat aboard with Peter, he was wondering aloud what she would be like if she were 10 instead of seven tons when his wife snapped, "You've grown out of her."

Maurice had to agree and immediately began searching again for another boat. Both he and Peter stumbled across a large smack-yacht in the saltings above Paglesham.

She seemed ideal - like a larger *Storm*.

"She's a proper ship," Peter stated.

"Do you like her?" asked Maurice cautiously.

"Well, she's a hefty looking boat. Bit of a handful for one."

"Yes ... but for two?" asked Maurice.

"I think she's rather fine. You could grow to love a ship like this." Peter's remark in the third person was enough for Maurice who thought, "... perhaps if I had a boat this size, one that would really suit two, and one more like my wife's idea of a cruiser, it might be that she would share it with me ... some time."

Ever hopeful of a sailing partnership with his wife, Maurice changed the 34ft Colchester smack's name from *Evadne* to *Afrina*. "Our old honeymoon ship," he told Peter.

The beamy (10ft 3in) old hull, built in 1898, was put off on a mooring for her new owner who invited Norman Clackson to join Peter and himself for the passage round to the Blackwater, where Peter was fitting out *Juanita* as usual in Heybridge Basin.

The River Roach was a froth of white horses, the January Saturday the trio arrived in Norman's Bentley. They stood on the leeward side of the large black barge-building shed on the sea wall and looked out across the moorings. The local boat builder, Frank Shuttlewood, stood with his stocky frame protected from the wind with jerseys and seaboots and said, "You'll want all your reefs in that mains'l today, Mr Griffiths."

"How deserted it looked, between the level banks of mud and waving sedge grass! It would have cheered us to have seen just one other boat in the anchorage. I am certain that the wind was blowing at gale force that day, and was the kind

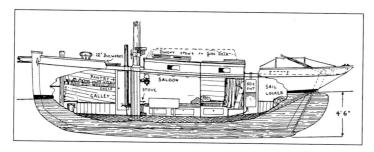

Afrina
(ex–Evadne)
had a roomy
layout below

of breeze that had a weight in it one would never find in a summer gale in May or June," Maurice observed.

With three reefs pulled down in the mainsail and the smallest jib aboard set, Afrina stiffly rolled a few inches to leeward and smashed off down river.

Peter insisted on fighting the heavy tiller.

Norman later remarked, "It was blowing the best part of a gale and by God she was heavy work. Maurice couldn't manage her on his own and there was no engine in this bloody great boat - he wouldn't put an engine in her because he would never spend any money at all on his boats. He put some paint on of course to sell them again at vast profit!"

Gybing round a bend in the river, the 26ft long, 5in diameter boom slammed the old boat down to leeward and Peter, wrestling with the tiller, said to Maurice, "I guess you've bitten off more then you can chew this time, old man."

In the Rays'n, freezing spray misted across the decks causing Peter to hide under the upturned dinghy, "where she looked for all the world like a young terrier peeping out from his dark kennel".

Norman took the helm and sang sea shanties. Maurice heated soup on the fo'c'sle stove.

Norman said later of Peter: "On this occasion she was fairly quiet and well behaved. But she had this domineering streak - certainly with Maurice on boats. She wanted to be captain of the boat, but, well, Maurice wanted to be captain of his boat ..."

The couple tried sharing the helm unsuccessfully as Maurice recalled: "We did work a scheme which of course didn't work out, of being skipper on alternate days. Well of course that soon broke down.

"She was very, very assertive in boats. She hated to be the crew."

Beating up the Blackwater, Peter likened Afrina to a submarine and Norman said, "What's the colour of the forehatch, Maurice? I'd go and see if I had my galoshes."

The crew of *Afrina* welcomed the relative peace and quiet of Mersea Quarters for the night, an anchorage where once the local chandler and broker, Bill Wyatt, had said to Maurice: "Why, Mr Griffiths, I do believe every time you bring up in Mersea you come in a different bo't!" Next morning they bashed on up to Heybridge.

Maurice found himself in a dilemma. *Afrina* was too heavy to handle alone, although he did manage to sail her once singlehanded, and yet Peter was not seduced by the ship. In fact, Maurice was beginning to understand she was not going to be seduced by any ship that was not her own.

"Being foolishly reserved, I had not found many 'free' shipmates whom I should like sailing with, and rather than have to endure week-ends with an uncongenial companion, I preferred to cruise alone.

"I had, at last, come to realise that *Juanita* was not a phase, a 'five year plan' as I had hoped at first, but a greatly loved fixture, and her owner, while intensely interested in my own ships, and ever willing to help me sail them at times, was not going to be parted from the ship into which so much of her personality had been infused ... in the light of later knowledge I cannot but smile at my own egotism and ingenuousness when I imagined that even *Juanita* would pass in due course."

Afrina

16

Head Winds

By the summer of 1931 Peter felt it was time Maurice should crew for her by way of a change and so he left *Afrina* in the hands of riggers for some new shroud lanyards and shipped aboard *Juanita* for a cruise to Holland.

The clumsy old boat floated out of Harwich and into the fog giving the couple some stressful hours listening to ships' hooters.

For 24 hours they had little or no wind while "every now and then patches of flotsam drifted into view, slipped by and were swallowed up astern, pieces of wood, boxes, half-submerged baskets, patches of weed, a medley of halves of grapefruit - a steward had thrown them overboard from some passenger vessel probably after breakfast - looking clean and fresh in the clear green depth of the sea. We looked for them, for they were our only connection with the outer world," Maurice observed.

He didn't like it. It bored him. He considered that people who made world voyages were "quite mad" and pined for a quiet creek where he could listen to the tide leaving the mud.

They eventually picked up the West Hinder lightship to find the wind heading them from their intended destination - Flushing. So Peter settled on Ostend instead.

Yet they could not weather Ostend either and faced another night, this time beating against a foul tide. Neither had eaten for the last eight hours - Peter had already been sick and Maurice had come close to throwing up in sympathy. A tot of whisky each eased their depression and fortified them to face the slog until dawn.

With the light they sailed exhausted into Ostend, 35 hours out from Harwich.

For three days they lay there weather bound as a sou'westerly gale lashed the Belgian coast; then they set sail for Flushing.

Outside the harbour an irregular swell rolled *Juanita*'s main boom into the sea and continually gybed her mizzen.

North Sea gale

"Peter's face was a study," Maurice later wrote. "'God, what a climate!' she almost screamed. 'Either a blasted gale or a flat calm! Just look at this swell!'"

Next they were forced below as torrential rain hit them off Zeebrugge.

Peter said, "I'll be as sick as a cat if I stop in here." She returned to the cockpit "looking like a disgusted young seal as she stood hunched up in her glistening oilskins".

They lost the fair tide and without any wind *Juanita* started to drift back towards Ostend.

"The flood's beginning," Maurice said, stating the obvious.

"The skipper glared at the receding shore a mile away and darted a look at the sky - the kind of look a woman would give a successful rival in a love affair," Maurice wrote.

"All right. LET go then. I suppose we'll roll our insides out here for the rest of the day!" Peter ranted.

At last a breeze came and *Juanita* made Flushing that evening.

Peter dressed herself up in immaculately pressed flannel trousers and reefer jacket complete with cheese cutter hat to visit the customs with the ship's papers as captain.

Her rig caused some amusement ashore. As she and Maurice wandered about exploring, a crowd of Dutch street urchins began to tag along.

"For heaven's sake," said Maurice. "I wish you'd put a skirt on, this is very embarrassing."

Years later, on reflection, Maurice said, "They'd never seen a woman in trousers before. Very few women wore shorts or trousers then and of course lots of people thought it was very queer, very queer indeed."

Juanita put in a leg back to Ostend and Belgium before the passage home.

After sailing in fog across the Scheldt and up the Belgian coast Peter was very confident of her navigation.

"'We ought to see Ostend piers in an hour's time, she said in a matter-of-fact, damn-you-Mr-Mate-I'm-skipper-aboard-this-ship kind of voice. 'Call me if there's any change', and disappeared below," Maurice wrote later.

Their trip back across the North Sea did nothing to shake Maurice's conviction that deep water sailing was for masochists. They encountered a westerly gale, were both violently sick and lost the dinghy. The same depression sank a French pleasure steamer off Ushant with the loss of 500 lives and caused structural damage ashore.

Back once more on the East Coast, *Juanita* sailed up the Orwell to Pin Mill.

"Glad to be back in your old river, mate man?" asked Peter.

He was.

Peter knew there was little chance of press-ganging her husband aboard again so she took the advice of veteran yachtsman Frank Cowper who, reading her pieces in the yachting press, had taken up correspondence with her. It had been his ambition, unfulfilled, to start a sailing school and now instead he urged Peter to do so, his last letter ending:

Juanita *1930,*
hove–to in
North Sea gale

A cadet learning to plot a course on the chart with Peter Gerard

"Good-bye now, and think of an old man sometimes."

She did and asked Maurice to help design some brochures to attract 'cadets' aboard *Juanita*. Armed with these and an advert in a national daily, Peter soon had female applicants joining her aboard *Juanita* for sailing lessons that took them across the estuary and down Channel.

Maurice chuckled to himself as he subbed Peter's accounts of her training voyages for 'Yachting Monthly'.

"It was a long name; took up her entire hull; what *could* it be? We drove to wind'ard of and passed her end on before a failing shaft of twilight revealed it

"*East Goodwin.*

"Good God! About quick ... we're over the Goodwin Sands ..."

After one hard passage coming into the Colne, when "Seventeen cautious barges lay huddled affectionately together off the watch tower like a crowd of cornered mules, their slanting sprits like long ears laid back apprehensively", Peter and her girls wore make-up courtesy of Neptune: "our skins and eyelashes were powdered stiff with hardened salt." After cleaning up, Peter likened her change of soaking socks and shoes for dry equivalents to having "a brand new pair of feet".

So Peter's maritime school paid for *Juanita*'s upkeep. She became a hard case as she moved around in her man's world. At chandlers she would test 'brass' fittings with a magnet to make sure they were not just dipped steel.

She tore into anyone making a nautical cock up - once berating an astonished yachtsman who scoured *Juanita*'s topside while clumsily getting underway at Pin Mill, as an "idiot" and discovering later he was a friend of Maurice's.

She had started writing under a man's name because she didn't want to write as a woman. The few women who were sailing were to be found mainly in racing dinghies and they still wore skirts and blouses.

Now she failed to see that to be like a man she did not have to be aggressive and rude. She had her hair cut into an 'Eton crop'. Peter was becoming increasingly eccentric in her role as full time skipper. She was also rarely at home, which was now a house in Shenfield, Essex, where the railway line from Liverpool Street branched and thus gave access to all the East Coast stations as well as London.

One of the problems for this yachting man and wife team was that Maurice had now great responsibilites bringing out 'Yachting Monthly'; increasing its circulation; making sure the contents were fresh and well written. He was therefore restricted to weekends to get out on the water and often didn't even make those.

This did not suit Peter at all. She had always hankered after making a round-the-world voyage. When a young Australian woman turned up at the offices of 'Yachting Monthly' to tell of her voyage from Down Under to England aboard the four masted barque *Herzogin Cecilie*, Peter had found a soul mate.

Maurice remembers the sailor as a "quaint little thing in Edwardian clothes" and, significantly, that her father was the station master at one of the stops on the line across the Nullarbor Plain. He knew when a train was coming, Maurice recalled, because he could see the smoke four hours before the engine arrived.

After meeting this woman, Peter had been fired with the desire to make a passage in a clipper ship, but now such ambitions seemed very unlikely ever to be realised. So she made up for it with her frequent trips in *Juanita*. The thought of being a weekend sailor disgusted her.

"She couldn't think or talk about anything else but sailing," said Maurice later. "She didn't want any home life."

Peter also much preferred the Channel waters to the

irksome mudbanks of the Walton Backwaters.

"She wasn't interested in shallow water sailing as I am and we differed on a lot of points like that," he added.

Still, they had covered many nautical miles together and, despite their differences, Maurice dedicated his next book to her, but also to someone who had rather taken his berth aboard *Juanita*.

His classic book, 'The Magic of the Swatchways', was first published in 1932 and was inscribed:

"To PG and GN who understand these things."

Gwen Nevill was one of Peter's first and best cadets. Though 10 years her senior she became a good friend and a competent crew.

Maurice, many years before, had borrowed a book from Ipswich library called 'Swin, Swale and Swatchway' by H L Jones and published in 1892. The author with his boat *Tern*, based at Leigh-on-Sea, cruised much of the Essex and Kent creeks later explored by Maurice.

"That book certainly gave me the idea that if you collect a few cruising stories you could make a book of it. I really don't know what the ingredients were to have attracted people so much to 'The Magic of the Swatchways'. I wish I did," Maurice comments today.

Before 'Magic' the East Coast, or rather the Thames Estuary, had very few sailing yachts in its creeks - apart from those at Burnham-on-Crouch and Pin Mill - compared to the great yachting waters of the Solent and the Clyde.

"The yachting people in those days didn't think of it as anything," Maurice explains. "But here it was, a jolly nice cruising ground.

"I really can't say what the fascination is with sailing around mud and shoals and sands and narrow places. All I can say is that it has always fascinated me. You can't just sail around as you like as in deep water. You have to keep to the channels and swatchways.

"Sailing in places like that is similar to solving a puzzle ..."

17

Divorce

The shipwrights at Brookes' yard on Oulton Broad had been left with specific instructions to prepare Maurice's new boat *Nightfall* for his comfort in the early months of 1932. He had told them to fit a Jack Tar coal stove in place of the commode in her cabin, and they were to leave a 6in gap beneath its base to accommodate and keep warm his deck shoes!

The gaff cutter, built in 1910 was 31ft long, 9ft in the beam and had a 3ft 3in draught. The nine tonner had no centreboard and Maurice had found her long keel made her awkward in short tacking when he sailed her down from Acle.

In Easter that year Peter "tore herself away from her various maritime interests" to help sail *Nightfall* back to the Blackwater. The passage included a night sail across a bitter easterly wind. Peter found it too cold on deck, but the fug below made her seasick. When daylight found them becalmed off Bawdsey Haven they wallowed in a dying swell, "... while the mate, who had now revived, sat at the helm and cursed each of the elements in turn."

It was the last passage they made together.

Maurice was now busier than ever. He had set aside three nights a week to write - his third book 'Ten Small Yachts and Others' was published in 1933 - and weekends found him back at the drawing board with his designing.

Peter meanwhile was ever more involved with her cadets, sailing with two at a time, frequently down to the Solent and away from the hated mudbanks of the East Coast. She was away so often that Maurice found himself lumbered with domestic duties on top of his work load. It was perhaps inevitable that another woman was soon 'on his arm'.

Peter later described her marriage to 'Bungo' as "ideally happy", but added: "... an insidious rift developed in the lute by way of that time-honoured triangle-former, 'the other woman' who had already broken up one marriage, and later succeeded in breaking up another when she had finished with ours. Bungo managed ultimately to draw out in time to escape what would have been a mistaken union with her, but not soon enough to save us: since, metaphorically left alone to sort out my mangled emotions over some months, I had become a vulnerable target for the right kind of sympathy without consciously seeking it, being by temperament a one-man woman."

Recently widowed, the marine artist Chas Pears had taken a fancy to Peter whom he met regularly on her passages down to the Solent, where he kept *Wanderer*, the boat Maurice had sold him years earlier.

"Mixed loyalties ran disturbingly between the three of us, during which the fourth member, who had originated the impasse was nearly lost sight of. But as she recognised no loyalties she hardly counted except that in the aggravated circumstances Bungo and I finally decided we could not bring ourselves to surrender our new interests and start afresh," Peter wrote afterwards.

Maurice recalls: "She found domesticity very difficult. One could say those conditions rather led to the break-up of the marriage because I was a bit fed up to be left for a week or

Peter and Charles Pears aboard Wanderer *on the Cowes station (*Juanita *in the background)*

10 days at a time to help myself in the home."

At the time, Maurice's health went to pieces again and friends worried about him. Yet if Maurice were away and Peter were left alone, he would try to make arrangements to entertain her. Once during their time in Hampstead he asked Norman Clackson to take Peter out to dinner while he was away on business.

Norman said, "All she talked about was what she did in sailing. She wanted everything done her way. It was hopeless her marrying MG; she was hopeless at married life. He wanted to sail and she wanted to be captain of the ship and this didn't suit Maurice at all and obviously they rowed about this sort of thing."

Finally Peter moved into Chas Pears' studio in London's Holland Park.

"I think he was about 20 years older than my wife, but they were obviously very much in love. It was an amicable affair and in fact if anything, rather a relief on my part," Maurice reflects.

"It had been pretty disastrous. She was attractive physically and should have been a wonderful shipmate, but she wanted to be skipper all the time and I didn't care for that. She upset a lot of people. She used to fly off the handle at people and have hellish rows. It was rather embarrassing to find she'd had a storming row with somebody you knew quite well, a yacht owner or someone like that. She was very obstreperous.

"I ought never, never to have fallen for Peter in the first place, but there it is, one does these things."

There had been an occasion when Peter returned to the Hampstead flat one evening, having been taken by a little baby on the Tube.

"I'd like a little bugger like that," she told Maurice.

"But it was just in passing. It didn't mean anything. There was no marriage in it, or companionship or anything ...," Maurice remembers.

They divorced in 1934 and Peter married Chas Pears.

"He was a good bit older, a tough Yorkshireman who would stand no nonsense and although he was very much in love with her he could manage her, which I couldn't," comments Maurice.

Norman says, "Maurice was terribly worried about publicity; would it do any harm? Divorce wasn't as general then as now. He was very nervous. I suppose he thought from a yachting point of view it might be picked up in the press."

Peter's custom of habitually wearing trousers was in part due to her dislike of appearing as a nautical trollop. There were few women sailing in the 1930s and those who were seen aboard yachts were unfairly dismissed as the skipper's carnal comfort.

Men advertised in 'Yachting Monthly' for female crew. To make sure the magazine did not find itself acting as an unwitting dating agency, Norman Clackson ordered his secretary to probe the requests discreetly.

"There was an old Commander somebody who was rather notorious for this and we didn't want to get entangled in that," he says.

One advertiser seeking a woman crew sent the name and address of a person for a character reference after being subjected to the questionnaire of Norman's secretary.

"I wrote to this other fellow and I just got a short, rather polite letter back which said, 'As far as I'm aware John Smith's sexual habits are perfectly normal'. Which didn't help me very much!" said Norman.

For Christmas 1934 Maurice took himself off to Portugal aboard a steamer from Southampton. A solicitor friend, Alex Glen, worked for a legal company with a branch in Lisbon and Maurice delighted in some sailing on the Tagus in a Cape Cod cat boat with a wooden centreboard, which proved perfect for the shallow, sandbank infested upper reaches.

Maurice approved of the boat's finely-balanced board. The skipper could hold the board lifting lanyard in his fingers when beating up a narrow swatch. When the lanyard went slack the board had touched and thus the boat was put about.

"It was almost automatic, more definite than the ubiquitous echo sounder of today's yachts, and in the dark far less trying on the eyes."

While in Portugal, Maurice was able to indulge his other love - he was given an official permit to travel on the footplate of the locomotive hauling the Lisbon-Oporto express. At Quimbro where the railway workshops were based he was given a conducted tour by officials.

The holiday was such a success he repeated it two years later.

It had been five years since Maurice tried his first offshore race in the Fastnet. He did not like being offshore very much and he did not like racing, full stop. But when the celebrated designer Laurent Giles invited him as one of a four-man crew aboard *Etain*, a 12 ton bermudian sloop designed by Giles, Maurice's eclectic approach to life would not let him turn the opportunity down.

The boats set off from Burnham-on-Crouch for the Royal Corinthian Estuary Race - 90 miles round the great estuary sandbanks. The wind was already strong from the SSW and soon *Etain* had four reefs pulled down.

"Wet to the skin and sick at almost regular intervals, I found even the two-hour tricks at the helm trying, although the return to shiver in the cold comfort of the saloon, once more to experience the periodic miseries of sickness below decks, was scarcely more enjoyable," Maurice recalls.

After a day and a night *Etain* went ashore on the Red Sand much to the fury of the skipper.

"Just the opportunity for breakfast," Maurice said and the crew looked at him as though he were demented.

The hot food gave them fresh heart, however, and back at Burnham they discovered they had won. All the other boats had retired.

It was enough to put Maurice off racing for more than a decade!

His next venture in competitive sailing was in 1948 for the RORC Channel race from Cowes to Dinard aboard *Erivale*, a 26 ton Robert Clark racer. The following year Maurice shipped aboard a 32ft bermudian cutter, *Sixpence*, for the RORC North Sea race from Harwich. All the crew was sick, the skipper actually vomiting blood before they retired. Maurice never went racing again.

"I never did have any notable or praiseworthy experiences in RORC races. What experiences I did have usually put me off racing for the next few years!" Maurice says with feeling.

18

Marinas and Flying Boats

When Maurice wrote about *Nightfall* for the YM series 'The Other Man's Boat' in 1933, the only real complaint he had was that her cockpit sidebenches prevented the crew from being able to rinse saucepans over the side! This he altered, inserting an athwartship bench so he could steer with one arm lazily draped over the tiller and a cushion at his back.

One of the first of his now exclusively male crew to sail with him aboard *Nightfall* was his good friend Henry 'Morty' Mortimore with whom he had nearly drowned on the Gunfleet. Another was Bill Elliston, an old school chum, who had sailed with Maurice in *Storm*.

During one cruise the pair sat birdwatching on the mud behind Havengore and Maurice followed Beatrix Potter's style of clothing fauna in human garb.

Nightfall, 31ft cutter, 1910. Owned by MG 1932/36

As the pair watched a heron - "The motionless statue, like that of a little old man in a grey frock coat, suddenly darted at the water, and with a flurry of outstretched wings, sailed upward and away, a fish clutched in his beak and his long legs stretched out behind him" - Maurice asked Bill whether he would feel 'nobler' at that moment smashing his way across the North Sea to a foreign country.

He would not. Yet Maurice had been hurt

Nightfall *with MG at the helm*

by Peter's dismissal of him as a mud-hopper. He took comfort in reminding himself of other illustrious yachtsmen who were as happy as he with the Thames Estuary – Francis B Cooke for example, the yachtsman and author of many books on sailing. He had agreed with Maurice that, with the one odd cruise now and again 'to the other side' in a friend's yacht, he was quite content to spend his long life (he died aged 103) in the rivers between the North Foreland and Orfordness.

With Bill, Maurice sailed into Leigh-on-Sea to retrace the voyage of *Tern,* the boat that had inspired 'Swin, Swale & Swatchway', the book which, in turn, had inspired 'The Magic of the Swatchways'.

Mooring *Nightfall* up alongside Bell Wharf the pair employed a loafing longshoreman to keep an eye on the boat while they trudged through the little fishing village for a pint in the snug bar of the ancient 'Peter Boat' pub.

En route Maurice looked in at Bundock's boat shed where his beloved *Storm* had been built.

"... looking like many another old boatyard, with stacks of timber seasoning in the open, weathered moulds like mock-up bulkheads from various craft built here stacked against a wall, a big tarred weatherboarded shed with a leaky corrugated roof, and through a doorway inside the ecclesiastical gloom of a church where there was a pervading smell of freshly sawn pine, wood shavings, paint and pitch."

After lunch they bought half a pound of Maurice's favourite sandwich filling, smoked cod's roe, from one of the cockle-cooking sheds, and sailed away to the East Swale where Bill could indulge his own fond memories of *Storm.*

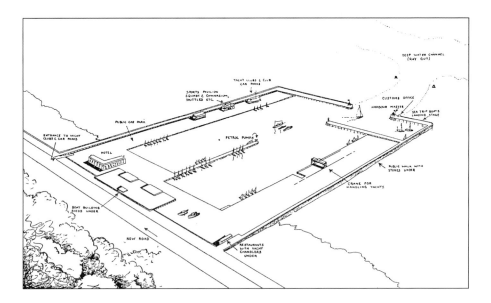

The proposed yacht harbour at Chalkwell Bay, Southend

It was to the Swale Maurice later took two South Coast yachtsmen he'd met through YM. They could not believe the peace and space of the East Swale anchorage, which has changed little even at the time of writing.

One of them said, "Why, an anchorage like this near the Solent would be *packed* with craft, complete with gramophones and outboard motors." *Nightfall* was actually bound away to France, but his crew were so taken with the river that Maurice sailed them further up to Conyer, where at the 'Ship Inn' the threesome sat enjoying "cold meat and ale".

After many hours becalmed in a "vile oily swell" they did eventually cross to Dunkerque with the crew complaining that *Nightfall* did not have an engine.

Soon after that Maurice had a Morris Cowley 'Bullnose' car engine installed in order to make the most of his annual 10 day holiday.

After almost 10 years at the helm of 'Yachting Monthly', Maurice had increased the circulation by many hundreds, but ever aware how fickle fortune could be, wanted it up further. His old beliefs in making sailing as popular as possible led him to support plans for an early marina.

On the editorial page, 'The Watch Below', Maurice backed calls by a consortium to build a £250,000 "first class yacht harbour" at Chalkwell Bay on the Southend shoreline. How many boat owners, introduced to the 'magic' Maurice discovered from his own mud-larking, had craft moored within the proposed marina's boundary, is not recorded.

Maurice promised such a scheme would make Southend like Florida! He claimed yachtsmen would buy houses in Southend to be near their craft and "settle down" there.

"Much, of course, would depend on improved social attractions in the district from the residential point of view.

"Such a harbour would prove a tremendous benefit to Southend itself. A vast amount of money would be spent locally by the yachting communities, and in place of the childish and costly coloured illuminations which the local ratepayers have to bear in the summer, and which only bring to Southend an undesirable element on daily trips from the East End of London, with no money to spend, this yacht harbour would attract visitors of a more satisfactory class," he snootily wrote.

It would also boost the potential readership of 'Yachting Monthly'. "It is solely the lack of reasonable convenience and easy facilities that prevents yachting and motor boating becoming one of our largest industries," he added.

Not long after this controversial editorial, Maurice exhibited a NIMBY (Not In My Backyard) attitude. Norman Clackson introduced Maurice to an old friend, Norman Jones, a flying ace. He expressed great enthusiasm for using Hamford Water in Maurice's precious Walton Backwaters as a runway for flying boat trips.

"You should have seen Maurice's face. He was horrified with the idea," said Norman. He let his objections be known and the Royal Yachting Association soon squashed the plan.

Maurice said, "Think of those things touching down and taking off in Hamford Water. They are so big and noisy they would have been far worse than the ski-boats you get today."

Maurice tired of *Nightfall*, not because she didn't suit him, in fact with the possible exception of *Storm* she was the best boat he had owned to date, but because he now had the ability and the wherewithal to design and have built his own yacht.

Maurice had a 400 mile cruise in the Hebrides aboard *Rawanah*, a 35ft double ender he had designed for a customer wanting a good seaboat.

Surrounded by awesome soundings he literally felt out of his depth. "I looked around with almost a sense of apprehension at the still bay [East Loch Tarbert] with its overhanging rocks and dank sea-weed, the silent phalanxes of the trees and the impenetrable shadows in their depths, at the grim turret of the castle peering over the tops of the pines, and above all at the unfathomable water that lay still and

Wild Lone II,
10 tons, 1935

ominous beneath our keel. There were shadowy forms of
immense jellyfish far down, like ghostly shapes, moving
slowly, and as I coiled the lead line it stung my hands as
though it had plunged deep into some submarine hell where
even the water itself was rank and poisonous."

Maurice was so impressed with *Rawanah*'s seakindliness
that in designing his own first yacht he rather overlooked the
lessons he had learnt about shoal draught. *Wild Lone II* was
certainly a beautiful yacht, built by Harry King at Pin Mill
where the first *Wild Lone* had fitted out more than 10 years
before, but she was 4.8ft deep, rather more than Maurice had
come to believe was ideal for estuary cruising.

The 35.6ft bermudian yawl had almost identical
underwater lines to those of *Rawanah*.

As Maurice watched Harry's men winch her slowly down
into the tide at Pin Mill in 1936, he likened the launch to a
bridegroom's doubts on his wedding day and thought, "Good
heavens, MG, what have you done? She's not a bit your
type!"

It was almost as if subconsciously he were still trying to
convince his old partner to come sailing with him. The boat
seemed designed in spite of himself, for *Wild Lone II* would
have pleased Peter much more than she did Maurice: "...
another of my mistakes," he wrote ambiguously later.

There was to be little time to sail her anyhow. Maurice was
now turning his hand to fiction writing, hoping to hit the
jackpot with a bestseller. His first novel, 'Dempster and Son',

followed the loves and lives of two generations of railway engineers and gave Maurice great pleasure in the research. His second, 'No Southern Gentleman', was an American Civil War romance. He was also still compiling nautical books. Including 'Little Ships and Shoal Waters', 'Cruising Yarns from the YM' and the novels, he had no fewer than four books published between 1937 and 1939.

In the autumn of 1937, 'Yachting Monthly' sent him to Newport, Rhode Island for a month to cover the America's Cup races. While there he spent all his spare time digging up more information on shoal draught boats. He talked with Nat Herreschoff the celebrated US designer, Olin and Rod Stephens of Sparkman Stephens fame and Alf Loomis. He also found inspiration in the models room of the New York Yacht Club.

It all led him to the conclusion that he was on the right course - good shoal draught boats were probably better than deep yachts in heavy weather.

With holiday cruises to destinations as different as Madeira and Helsinki, there was no time left for sailing *Wild Lone II* any distance and she was proving unsuitable for moorings at Heybridge on the Blackwater. Ironically she was sold to a Scotsman who took her back to the waters of the Hebrides where she had been a twinkle in Maurice's eye.

Many years later, in the summer of 1992, this shapely yawl, renamed *Wild Goose* and under the ownership of the late Miles Clark (a former YM journalist) made a record voyage by way of the Lofoten Islands and North Cape to the White Sea, Archangel and through the rivers of central Russia to the Black Sea and Istanbul. This was a route never before attempted by a foreign yacht.

A drawing board had long been installed at Maurice's Shenfield home and many of his designs were deliberately made as economical as possible to fit the YM reader's pocket.

Norman said, "Maurice must have made a lot of money on his boat plan business because they were selling all the time. He had brought 'Yachting Monthly' down to the 10 ton yacht maximum market."

Maurice published his own designs in YM along with many others from different designers.

"We never published boats that we thought were bad designs, bad shapes. From the 1930s onwards there were several pretty good amateur designers, and we published them, including the very excellent work of Harrison Butler. Occasionally I would slip in a design of my own," says

Lone Gull

Maurice.

He had got the circulation up to 7,000 towards the late 30s. At that time all the competing yachting magazines had circulations no higher than 5,000.

Designed for comfort rather than speed, *Lone Gull* was built by Johnson & Jago at Leigh-on-Sea in 1938. Deep in Maurice's sub-conscious were the lines of the boat he had coveted as a boy when he gazed at *Scoter* in The Bight at Ipswich, for when boat builder Len Johnson looked at Maurice's plans for his new boat, he immediately recognised *Scoter* and said as much.

There was much about *Lone Gull*, a bermudian cutter, which reflected Maurice's researches in America - her L-shaped centreboard made from 2in oak planks and her beamy hull form in particular.

Yet she was not a success. Maurice candidly admitted her plate was too far aft for decent windward performance, her stern was too full for downwind speed - he had designed it that way to fit in the engine - and the mast was stepped on the keel through tongue and groove, canvas covered decks, which opened up whenever the shrouds slackened, allowing the mast to lever them apart.

Nevertheless four of these 28ft 6in x 10ft x 3ft boats were built, one of them sailing across the Atlantic to the West Indies, where she was used on charter.

Before Maurice had a chance to offload her, Hitler marched into Poland and the world changed forever.

Selina Griffiths sailing Lone Gull I *in the Orwell 1939 (aged 73)*

19

Mine Patrol

The rough wooden hull of the old steam drifter nosed its way uncertainly through the flat watery acreage of the Rays'n Channel. Up on the bridge Maurice Griffiths glanced nervously at the 'signpost' Buxey Beacon with its four fingers warning seafarers off the high bank it marked.

There was water, water everywhere, but not enough, or so it was looking, to float the 11ft 6in of planking that lurked below the waterline of *Sailor King*.

Up by the trawl gantry a member of the crew swung the heavy shackle on the end of the leadline (the lead itself had probably been swiped by some longshore scoundrel) into the brownish tide.

"Two and a half fathoms," he shouted.

Maurice looked over to starboard. There was water between *Sailor King* and the seawall over two miles away, but he knew that very few feet below its deceptive surface the Dengie Flat lay waiting.

It was high water. Soon the sluggish surface would start moving in a huge sheet off the land.

"Just over two fathoms," cried the lead-swinger. Maurice flinched.

"I hope you know what you're doing Griff," came the growling voice of Commander Bill Hamond, who was aboard for the 'ride'. "Because if anyone is going to be court-martialled for this, you know, it'll be me!"

"One and three quarter fathoms."

Suddenly *Sailor King* felt different.

"Damn," muttered Maurice under his breath as her head swung off to port. "We've touched."

Maurice rang the engine room for 'dead slow'. *Sailor King*'s stern lifted a few inches and she was afloat once more.

It was now a juggle between keeping maximum speed on to get over the shallow southern end of the Rays'n before the tide started to ebb and yet keep her stern from dipping down

*Lieut
M W Griffiths
RNVR
aboard
HM Trawler
Sailor King,
August 1940*

through too many revs.

When *Sailor King* had got orders to investigate a suspected unexploded mine seen in the River Crouch, she had been lying at Brightlingsea. Maurice had done some fast calculations and worked out that his not-so-little ship would have a foot to spare if he timed it right.

While that was plenty of water for an East Coaster like Maurice, Commander Hamond, who built dinghies in his back garden at Porchester, Hants, was a South Coast man who did not like mud.

He never forgot his trip through the Rays'n and recounted the passage many years later to his goddaughter Jenifer and her husband Brian Brooke-Smith.

Brian repeats the tale that "Mercifully the silent prayers of both of them were answered and they were suddenly into deep water and able to proceed at full speed up the Crouch. The mutual congratulations which were then exchanged at having saved a good two hours on the passage became quite euphoric - and neither of them dwelt on the final estimate of the depth of water actually beneath the ship's keel at a mere two inches!"

Maurice and Norman Clackson had both joined the Royal Naval Volunteer (Supplementary) Reserve following the Chamberlain crisis in 1938. Dubbed the 'spare time sailors', the RNVR, or 'Wavy Navy' as it was also known because of the undulating rings and braid as opposed to the straight versions of the RN that the uniforms sported, began with 1,000 officers and 7,000 ratings.

Encouraged by the Treasury - signing up yachtsmen who already had boathandling and navigation experience saved them a fortune in training - the RNVR supplied 80 per cent of the Royal Navy's officers by the end of the war.

When the war started in September 1939 both Maurice and Norman were called up.

Maurice was appointed as a Sub-Lieutenant to HMS *Vernon* at Portsmouth to the Enemy Mining Section. He was trained in defusing the magnetic mines being dropped on parachutes by the enemy over the East Coast and the channels of the

Thames Estuary.

Oddly enough Maurice had already gained a fundamental knowledge of mines while researching for his book 'No Southern Gentleman' about the American Civil War. He had discovered the Confederate forces used well caulked kegs stuffed with gunpowder against the blockading Yankee ships, as well as controlled mine fields at harbour entrances connected to electric batteries ashore.

The Admiralty was very concerned at the loss of four to five ships a day to these mines and was desperate to find a mine intact, defuse it, take it apart and discover how it worked. Only then could an antidote be found.

The very waters which Maurice had found sanctuary in were now ideal for mine warfare because they were shallow. A method of dredging these mines using special non-magnetic trawls to haul them onto a beach and render them safe was soon developed. Steam trawlers were commandeered by HMS *Vernon*, but after one, *Mastiff*, was blown up while retrieving a mine near the Tongue in the Thames Estuary with the loss of half her crew, some older steam drifters with wooden hulls, offering greater protection against the magnetic pull of the mines, were converted with the special trawling gear.

HMT Scotch Thistle *overhauls HMT* Sailor King, *1940*

They were sent on patrol in groups of four as HMS *Vernon* Mine Recovery flotillas, with Commander Hamond, RN, in command.

Maurice was promoted to Lieutenant, appointed group officer of MRF3, whose area of duty was the east coast as far north as Aberdeen.

The fleet were *Frons Olivae, Scotch Thistle, Achievable* and his own *Sailor King*.

The summer of 1940 was, as history records so vividly, a fine one and Maurice enjoyed working a small craft around the coast, thinking to himself it was as close to steam-yachting as he was likely to come.

But that trip up the Rays'n was a close call.

"My God it was foolish of me. I know it was a big spring tide, but you could feel her touch if we speeded up. If we had dried out there, my godfathers, oh dear, oh dear," Maurice still recalls the time with embarrassment.

"It would not have taken us much longer to have gone through the Spitway, but I have always rather loved the Rays'n ... it was a foolish piece of navigation and needless to say we didn't come back that way."

Having had a false alarm to join the convoys of small craft going to Dunkirk, *Sailor King* and her flotilla were re-routed back to their base at Dundee. Soon the Tay was declared free of mines and the drifters were brought further south and based in Lowestoft, which suited Maurice.

When *Sailor King* was engaged in salvaging an RAF bomber, which had ditched in Corton Road between Lowestoft and Great Yarmouth, Maurice met and befriended RNVR Lieutenant Rex Sullivan. They got on so well that the pair agreed to set up a salvage business after the war.

Sadly it was not to be. Rex was sent to Falmouth to check up on another German mine, but it exploded while he was diving round it and he and the boat crew were killed.

In September that year London was blitzed and HMS *Vernon*'s Mine Rendering Safe parties were rushed to the capital to clear the London docks and East End, which had been carpeted with unexploded parachute landmines.

Maurice's shift worked non-stop for 10 days and nights.

"It was nasty work indeed. A fair number of chaps got killed when things blew up on them. I was lucky. Mostly I had to clear areas and blow the darn thing up."

For his part in the Blitz, Maurice was awarded the George Medal. The notice of this award appeared in 'The London Gazette' dated Friday, 10th January 1941, where the entry read simply: 'The KING has been graciously pleased to approve the award of the George Medal for gallantry and undaunted devotion to duty, to Temporary Lieutenant Maurice Walter Griffiths, R.N.V.R.' No further detail was given as to the reason for the award and Maurice himself remains as tight lipped as a Mersea oyster on the specifics.

Sailor King continued in her mine recovery work. Once the parachute mine was located it was hooked up in the trawl and towed towards the beach. Then with a snatch block fixed ashore, the former fishing boat's steam winch was used to drag the mine ashore.

"They were nasty looking things - bull-nosed at one end with a four fin tail at the other. The parachutes had 24 to 28 silk cords."

Maurice, now a Lieutenant Commander, found himself more of a hero among the ladies for his generous distribution of these straps, which were used as dressing-gown cords, than for his medal!

Of Maurice's flotilla only *Sailor King* and *Scotch Thistle* survived.

One of the others was blown to pieces while working on a magnetic mine in shallows off Margate; the other was damaged beyond repair after colliding with a freighter in the Thames one night.

Mines kept on raining down - the Germans were now targeting docks and harbours around Britain. To combat this the Navy stepped up its training of divers to seek and defuse underwater mines perilously close to valuable installations or large ships. In order to be put in command of such a team, Maurice was sent to Whale Island in Portsmouth Harbour for a crash course in diving. This was before the time of the aqualung and Maurice found himself 160 lb heavier, dressed in the lead weights, brass boots, and brass helmet supplied with the standard diving outfit as he plodded along the bottom of Portsmouth Harbour breathing air supplied through pipes from the surface.

Sailor King

20

Suez Duties

The combination of shallow water and bottleneck provided the enemy with what could have been one of its most effective strategies - mining the Suez Canal. And the one man who knew about shallow water and mines was soon aboard a stripped out Wellington bomber en route to Ismailia to deal with the latest threat. Already two ships had been sunk and were blocking the canal.

Maurice quickly found two old trawlers and had them converted for mine surfacing, but one day he received a report that a parachute mine had been checked over by a diver who had noticed it was different in construction from those so far dealt with.

Maurice and his diving crew set sail for the channel at the southern end of Lake Timsah. He had decided to dive himself on the mine. He was however talked out of it by one of his crew - the diving suit was oversize and the crew member, known as 'Lofty', was a head taller than Maurice.

Maurice and the crew sat fidgeting in the boat as they watched Lofty's carbon dioxide bubble to the surface.

When he surfaced holding the priming charge and detonator, all aboard heaved a sigh of relief. Then back at base Maurice was met by a cypher officer who handed Maurice a signal from the Admiralty which read:

"Diving on to unexploded mines with intention of rendering safe under water is to cease forthwith. Anti-stripping device is now being fitted to cause mine to detonate on primer chamber being flooded. All diving parties are to be informed."

Maurice handed the signal back and muttered, "Oh well, you live and learn - if you live."

He had a similar experience a few months later in May 1941 when a mine splashed into the canal at Toussoum, 12 miles south of Ismailia. The converted trawler *Landfall* steamed straight to the spot and, having engaged the ordnance with her copper nets, started 'trawling' it up the bank.

This time the mine was much heavier and the trawler failed to winch it completely clear of the water, so a six-wheeled truck was also used and it was hauled up on to the canal-side road.

The mine was found to have two small windows on its side. They were not large enough to be inspection plates and the recovery team were puzzled as to their purpose.

A robot 'trepanner' was placed on the side of the mine and while Maurice and his crew stood at a safe distance it cut out a hand-sized hole.

After all the team had peered inside the mine, a dispatch rider turned up, who informed them that the as yet unexploded mine in front of them was a state-of-the-art 'bomb-mine', whose windows were photoelectric cells and part of an anti-recovery device!

While out in Egypt, Maurice had a couple of pleasant interludes, which took him back to the trouble free and now so distant times of his yachting past.

He met the Commodore, Colin Marshall, of the yacht club in Alexandria, for whom he had designed the 30 ton centreboard ketch *Ionia*, 10 years before. Marshall was delighted with his boat, which he described as "my dream ship" and invited Maurice for a cruise in the Eastern Mediterranean after the war.

He also ran into Norman Clackson in Cairo, who told him he had been sunk off Tobruk when his ship had been blown up by ... a magnetic mine.

Suffering from malaria and dysentery, Maurice came home from Egypt in January 1942 for some well earned leave. Sick as he was Maurice never forgot the flight back to Portsmouth, for he returned in a Shorts Sunderland seaplane, flying over Lake Victoria, Stanley Falls and Leopoldville to Lagos on the west coast of Africa, where he spent eight days. From there he flew to Ireland in another seaplane, an American Clipper, and finally to Portsmouth in a Royal Navy plane.

Back at HMS *Vernon* he discovered the mine recovery flotillas had been all but dispersed following the success of reducing ships' magnetic influence by degaussing, so he was drafted into the Explosives and Demolition Department, where his editing experience was put to use updating the Navy's Demolition Handbook.

This work led Maurice to head the preparation for a secret operation, the details of which were not disclosed to him. His brief was simply that he must prepare charges to scuttle 77 ships in shallow water.

They must not be holed too far below the waterline as they were to remain upright and their hulls were to be filled with ballast, which should not be washed out by tidal action.

Maurice set to work on his task and early tests were made on two wrecks - one a ship that had been mined off Gravesend, another on a vessel off the Dorset coast.

Soon he had a list of the condemned ships. They lay in ports all over the UK from Cardiff to the Clyde, Southampton to the Manchester ship canal and Tilbury to Londonderry.

To visit each ship proved extremely difficult. Trains were disrupted by bunkering raids, the Navy had no small planes available and Maurice's request for a staff car driven by a spare, in the best sense of the word, Wren were dismissed.

So he contacted an old pre-war sailing friend, Arnold 'Tubby' Watson OBE. Tubby was chief test pilot for the Air Transport Auxiliary, a body set up by Gerard D'Erlanger to ferry pilots to and from aeroplane factories as the new fighters and bombers were rolled out ready for delivery to their respective RAF bases.

Tubby persuaded his boss that the Navy, in reality Maurice, had a problem getting to the scattered ships. Soon, under orders from HMS *Vernon*, Maurice was able to request an ATA flight to pick him up from Portsmouth Airport - then a field outside the town - and fly him to the port he had to visit.

The plane was usually an eight-seater Rapide and once Maurice and Tubby had a hair-raising flight through fog.

"It could be a bit dicey at times. If there was a raid on for instance we had to keep below a thousand feet in what was referred to as the 'liveable corridor'. Once we were flying in this corridor when fog shut down. We were groping our way along when suddenly a great sausage thing passed our wing and we realised we were below the barrage balloons. We just had to weave our way through. Fortunately we did otherwise I wouldn't be here!" Maurice recounts.

The condemned ships were codenamed 'Corncobs' and were all different. They ranged from a little 5,000 ton Norwegian steamer to an ex-German liner of 17,500 tons. The skill came in working out how much explosive was required to blow a hole no bigger than 3ft in diameter in different hull thicknesses.

There were tramp steamers with plates three-eighths of an

inch thick, cargo vessels with half-inch sides and a French
warship of the Dreadnought type built in 1911, the *Courbet*,
with hull plating an inch and a quarter thick. On the last,
slower expanding charges were designed to "give it time to
get through".

Each ship was supplied with its *Vernon* demolition party of
Naval ratings in the charge of an RNVR Lieutenant. The
number of scuttling charges varied from four each side in the
smaller ships to 10 a side in the *Courbet* and the German
liner.

All through 1943 Maurice flew to the different hulls,
making sure the correct charges were being fitted but it was
not until 6th June, 1944, that the world and Maurice
discovered a harbour had been built off the Normandy
beaches that would land the greatest invasion fleet in history,
beginning on D-Day.

Maurice's 77 scuttled ships formed a half-mile long
crescent, which acted as a breakwater to give shelter to the
pre-cast concrete boxes that constituted the Mulberry
harbours.

The Americans on Omaha beach were given about 20 of
the ships, but as Maurice discovered when he landed there a
week after D-Day, they were sunk much too far out and only
the upper works were above water at high tide, whereas the
idea had been for the upper deck, at least, to be above sea
level to provide shelter. This may well have had something to
do with the fact that the US forces encountered far hotter
resistance than the other allies.

As well as all his RNVR duties, Maurice nevertheless had
found time to keep on writing. He had a book prepared to
launch on a public sick and tired of war. 'Post-War Yachting',
published in 1945, had the preface datelined: HMS *Vernon*. It
began:

"Yacht cruising and yacht racing are not merely sports for
the favoured few; the recent war years proved how valuable a
body of trained yachtsmen can become to the Admiralty. Had
there not been such a body of keen sailing and motor-cruising
men in this country in 1939, men of the RNVR who were
ready and competent to man the minesweepers, the patrol
services, the coastal defence craft, the MLs, the MTBs and
MGBs, and above all the numerous landing craft in the
assaults on the enemy's mainland, it is difficult to say how
this country would have fared. It is indeed a solemn thought.

"The value of yachting as a training ground for war as
well as for defence was fully recognised by our enemies. All

U-boat commanders and the cream of the Luftwaffe pilots received a thorough training in seamanship and navigation aboard the large fleet of very fine yachts owned by the Kriegsmarine and the Luftwaffe and maintained for that purpose. The navies of other advanced powers also possess small sailing vessels for the training of their officers, while the Russian Admiralty has now followed suit by introducing Soviet-owned yachts for the gaining of naval experience. For national reasons alone, therefore, yachting is more than a pursuit of pleasure, and the British Admiralty is fully aware of the debt this country owes its yachtsmen."

21

Coppie

It had been 10 years since Maurice's divorce from Peter. He had lived with his mother in the Shenfield house and "I'd almost settled down and decided to call it a day - to admit I would remain a bachelor."

Then one day after lunch in the *Vernon* wardroom, Maurice was reading about the Allies' progress across Europe in the 'Daily Telegraph', when a chum whispered, "Have you seen our new Wren officer?"

Maurice peered over the top of the paper and "I thought 'This is it.'"

Second Officer Wren Marjorie Copson with her "quizzical eyes", was a Northampton lass four years Maurice's junior, who had never sailed before in her life. Her pastoral interests had been to do with horses and farm animals, but Maurice was no longer looking for a shipmate, he wanted a wife.

Off watch they packed their bicycles on the train and explored the countryside of Hampshire and Dorset. Marjorie remembers it as "gloriously unspoilt".

"Ours wasn't a glamourous love affair - more a comradeship," she says.

They were married at HMS *Vernon* in December 1944 and Marjorie, who soon insisted Maurice call her Coppie, as she loathed her Christian name, had her girls row the couple in a picket boat to the *Vernon* steps where two further lines of Wrens held crossed oars above their heads as they were welcomed aboard.

The send off to a brief honeymoon was taken care of by

Coppie at the time of her wedding, December 1944

Wedding day, 16th December, 1944. A group of Coppie's Boat Wrens gave a good send–off on the Vernon quay

Maurice's explosives team. The noise had every seagull in Portsmouth Harbour airborne.

The following year a book was published that covered a fictional marriage, that of David Creston who, if not Maurice's *alter ego*, then certainly, split between the other main character, Ian Martin, was a partly auto-biographical self-portrait.

The 'Sands of Sylt' was Maurice's last attempt at fiction. It is impossible not to compare it with Erskine Childers' 'Riddle of the Sands', a book that Maurice himself described as "prophetic", warning as it did of a German military threat coming from their low-lying Frisian Islands and being published before the First World War. It was almost irritating that Childers had got there first. If he hadn't written it, as like as not Maurice would have done, though as with 'Sands of Sylt', probably after the event.

Creston is a weedy, bespectacled, advertising copy writer, who meets his old friend Ian Martin, a swashbuckling yachtsman, in one of Maurice's old watering holes, 'The George', in Fleet Street. The period is mid 1930s.

Here Creston, whose only previous experience of sailing was the Broads, is invited to help Martin (they address each other, as was the protocol then, by surname) to sail his newly built yacht, *Solani*, home from Sweden.

Martin is an amateur boat designer who has won "at least one prize in a designing competition in a well known yachting monthly magazine".

Having arrived in Gothenburg, Creston learns more about Martin when he sees the boat and realises that he "had acquired the difficult art of designing successful yachts", which proved "that when he took to a subject he would not let it drop until he had completely mastered it".

Maurice goes on to describe Martin as "Taking life seriously, striving always to do the right thing" and Creston as being "attracted by the absurd, the ridiculous, the laughable aspect of human behaviour". For Creston life was "no straight road, no predescribed course between right and wrong, between duty and amusement", but instead "an adventure where anything goes, where every experience is to be welcomed, be it pleasant or disagreeable, where the mind is to be ever entertained by fresh happenings".

In summation Creston admits to himself the reason why he has come on such a cruise is to see how he would react to "tough, he-man, deep-sea cruising".

Soon Creston also discovers that Martin's widowed sister, Brenda Galpin, who has been at a finishing school in Heidelberg, is to accompany them for the passage home.

She comes aboard a "slender, sunburnt young woman wearing well fitting grey flannel slacks, brown canvas deck shoes and a brown sweater. With her fair hair cut in a trim shingle".

The first time Creston sees her at the helm, "her eyes sparkling, her long legs hidden in slacks and her knee-boots resting against the lee-coaming. She had one arm over the tiller, and her short fair hair was carried over to one side of her bronzed skin ..." She reminded him of a young Valkyrie on horseback. And everyone else of Peter Gerard!

The wimpish Creston is soon seasick to be nursed by Brenda offering him cups of Bovril!

Behind the 'Verboten' area of Sylt they see strange objects being dropped into the sea by Luftwaffe planes. Feeble Creston wins some respect from Martin by suggesting the reason the objects seem strange is that they are not humans.

"By gad, Creston maybe you're right. But if they're not men, what else could they be?"

"Bombs, bombs on parachutes," Creston wonders.

Later *Solani* is boarded by suspicious Gestapo officers, one of whom wonders if Martin is in the RNVR. "Is he not a Lieutenant in that excellent body of amateurs?"

To Creston's horror the German goes on to point out that the Thames Estuary routes, Black Deep and Princes Channel, are bottlenecks for shipping approaching London.

While Martin is determined to spy on the murky dealings of the Nazis behind the mysterious island of Sylt, Creston is equally determined to win the affections of Brenda: "So fair and slim and boyish, and yet so essentially feminine."

They eventually embrace and Brenda confesses: "All my life I've been something of a tomboy, wanting to do all the things my brother did."

Then when Creston admiringly praises her for being a competent yachtswoman she turns on him. "I detest the term yachtswoman. It belongs to 'Vogue' and Cowes Week."

Later, back aboard *Solani*, Martin gives orders for his crew to prepare sandwiches and fill the Thermos flasks with hot soup and cocoa, as they prepare to sail for England with his secret discoveries.

Creston feels inadequate about approaching Brenda again. "... I have always lacked that easy assuming manner with which many men break down a woman's defences. And women are as quick as children to detect shyness in a man and put up an appearance of impregnable resistance. Like a fool I can only think afterwards, far too late, how I should have gained confidence and overcome their reserve."

As a cathartic device to purge finally Peter Gerard from his soul, Brenda Galpin was a kind and gentle one, but when it came time for Brenda to consent "to become Mrs David Creston," Maurice drew the line. Peter Gerard suddenly became Coppie - "an absurdly young looking, black-stockinged Wren."

Once again, as in the 1914-18 war years the 'Yachting Monthly' was appointed the official journal of the RNVR, with an additional allocation of paper to enable it to keep going. Maurice's assistant, Kathleen Palmer, took over the editorial helm and through the six years of Blitz and shortages kept it going.

"Despite bombing raids, loss of materials by fire, shortages and delays occasioned by the Hitler war the magazine did not miss a single issue," says Maurice, whose curious phrase 'Hitler war' he used in later years instead of World War II, explaining that America's 'second war' was with Vietnam.

"And now we've had the Saddam War," he added.

Norman Clackson praised Kathleen Palmer's editorship. She had begun as Maurice's secretary.

"Without her help the whole thing would have gone bust. She was assisted by older contributors although she had a rather odd experience with E Keble Chatterton."

Keble Chatterton, a prolific maritime author, who also sailed and had written a yachtsmen's favourite, 'Down Channel in Vivette', was approached by Palmer to write a couple of articles for YM. They could be more or less about what ever marine subject he liked.

He wrote back saying, "My Dear Miss Palmer, I don't think we've been introduced have we?"

That was it.

Norman asked, "How do you cope with people like that?"

Peter Gerard was one of the old hands who did continue to contribute occasional articles.

Maurice gave all his spare time to help Kathleen Palmer

from *Vernon*. All letters addressed to him he answered, including one from a 14-year-old schoolboy, Dennis Bird, who wanted to make a model of *Wilful*. Maurice told him how to contact the new owners, by looking in Lloyd's List, and also sent him a printer's pull of her lines.

He also posted articles from *Vernon* and other stations around the UK to his old editorial office.

One was a nostalgic account of a cruise with Fid Harnack in *Lone Gull* in the summer of 1938. Fid teaches Maurice something about water colours, how in the hue of sea and sky, which to Maurice is slate grey, there is in fact much blue. At the end of their cruise the weather becomes finer and Fid takes *Hickey*, the dinghy, and rows away from a becalmed *Lone Gull* one morning as they drift through the Rays'n.

"So still was it, *Lone Gull* did not draw away from him, and a matchbox that I threw overboard remained within a few yards for over an hour," wrote Maurice.

Maurice is captured sitting on the cockpit coaming in the warm sun wearing nothing but a hat. Fid makes sure his painting is a stern view of both Maurice and *Lone Gull* and the result was published in the January issue of 1940.

The original still hangs in Maurice's study.

As *Lone Gull* heads back home towards the Nass, Fid accepts an offer to cruise to Holland the following year to sketch Dutch craft – a cruise that never happened as Maurice signs off in his piece:

Fid's drawing of Lone Gull *in the Rays'n*

"But when that next September came around and *Lone Gull* was all ready for her second little cruise, events in Europe changed all our lives, leaving the little ship laid up with a sad heart.

"But even war cannot take away the memory of those brief happy, idle days sailing for pictures."

22

Coppie Goes Afloat

As the war ebbed away many old yachts, which had been laid up for the intervening years, were found to be past it. Rot had set in and any timber available was being used to repair buildings. Other boats were never reclaimed. Nobody knew who owned them: perhaps their owners had died on some far flung battlefield.

Maurice 'salvaged' two from their wartime berths. *Keeyok*, a six ton centreboard sloop, and *Flamingo*, an eight ton gaff cutter, were in a weathered condition and, Maurice felt, unlikely to survive much longer. He bought both, had them re-fitted and sold them on to grateful owners.

Yet other yachts were damaged directly by the conflict. *Swan*, lying in Heybridge Basin, had her decks sprung by a Luftwaffe bomb. Even Maurice's *Lone Gull* lying at Leigh-on-Sea was covered in mud from another dumped German bomb.

Still, there was good news for the mass boating market, if not for the lovers of beautiful yachts. During the war a waterproof glue had been developed that made veneers of plywood impervious - eureka - marine ply had arrived and with it the DIY shipwright!

Maurice had by now designed 30 yachts and was an Associate of the Institution of Naval Architects, but post war conditions did not look good for freelance designing. He had written nine books, but memories of freelance hacking were still sore. Briefly Maurice considered taking a job in research for a railway company, but in the end he dismissed all the alternatives to the commuter train and returned to his old post back at YM, which had been kept open for him.

"There was a lot of change in the yachting business after the war, though it was stagnant for about the first three years. There were tight controls over materials and timber for yachts. You couldn't build a new yacht until about 1948. We kept up with the magazine of course, publishing articles and designs during that period. Then all of a sudden the yachting business took off. You could buy timber.

"Good waterproof plywood was what really made home building possible and the magazines started publishing plans for designs that used the material.

"One of the other yachting magazines published a how-to-build design and it was successful, so we followed suit."

The first was a half-decked 13ft 6in Junior class dayboat, which was so popular another was soon published, this time a 16ft version, the Senior, both from Kenneth M Gibbs.

Readers wanted bigger boats and so YM went on to commission the 19ft single chine *Wild Duck* and a 20ft three tonner, both from Alan Buchanan.

Coppie soon got to work transforming Maurice's Edwardian home at Shenfield. He was delighted, but also keen to teach his new wife how to sail. *Lone Gull* had not yet been refitted with her engine at Johnson & Jago's yard, but Maurice was so keen "to feel a tiller once more with my delightful bride beside me" that he told the yard to have the boat ready at least for a weekend sail - they could fit the engine the following week.

Thus Maurice took Coppie for her first ever sail down the winding Leigh Creek against a light easterly breeze on a falling tide. The inevitable happened and *Lone Gull* settled on the flats, just on the edge of the creek.

"No amount of hauling on kedges would get her off," recalls Maurice. "But she had a wide keel and settled almost upright on the hard shore."

To make sure she stayed put, Maurice unshipped a quant pole, a relic from the Broads-built *Nightfall*, from the starboard rigging, dug it into the mud and lashed *Lone Gull*'s rail to it, hoping it would act as a calliper.

"The breeze had almost died and all was peaceful as the tide ebbed away across the flats, except for ominous creaks now and then from the shrouds as though they were under great strain.

"Suddenly there was a loud crack as the quant pole broke and the yacht fell over to starboard on to the hard ground. With a cry Coppie fell out of her bunk on to the sloping floor.

"'She won't go any further' was my dismayed comment trying to think how the running tide must have scoured the ground from under the keel."

For a long while afterwards Coppie believed that was what all yachts did when they dried out.

Maurice did not take Coppie sailing on *Lone Gull* again until the engine was ready; instead Norman Clackson loaned

Maurice his own boat, *Gypsy*, for a few days.

"She was a kind, gentle boat," recalls Coppie. "And I enjoyed some quiet sailing on the Blackwater. This was going to be good, I thought."

But then Maurice, who had not raced offshore since his abortive Fastnet attempt with Peter 21 years before, received a tempting invitation from Dr Gordon Greville, who had entered his Shoreham based racer *Erivale*, 26 tons, for that year's RORC Channel Race to Dinard. Coppie would be a welcome companion aboard for Mrs Greville, he urged, thinking the ladies could take dresses to enjoy the dinner and jollities to follow.

Coppie joined *Erivale* at Cowes and stepped aboard with the owner's wife. A young man working on deck looked up and said, "Mother we can't take passengers on a race."

"This is my son, Nickie," said Mrs Greville quickly and hustled Coppie below.

"I still meet Nickie at the West Mersea Yacht Club," says Coppie. "And still feel somewhat embarrassed!"

Coppie was horrified the next morning as the race began in a Force 7 sou'wester.

"This was no gentle sailing and I soon became very frightened. *Erivale* was a true racing yacht. She heeled a lot," recalls Coppie.

The noise of the sails as she went about was deafening and Coppie found herself in the way as the crew hopped about letting go sheets.

When she came off watch, Coppie remarked, "I haven't seen a single ship's lights all night," to which the skipper replied, "No you wouldn't, we've been cutting across the minefields!"

Coppie recalls, "I soon had to retire below to my bunk, very sick and wet. Mrs G joined me, then the skipper and then the crew, leaving only Maurice and Nickie to sail."

Erivale returned to the Hamble.

That same year Maurice performed another rescue operation on one of his designs. *Zoraya*, a 14 ton bermudian ketch, had been built in Bombay in 1946, but before her launch in 1947 her owner had a heart attack and was advised to give up sailing.

Zoraya was shipped home from India and deposited at Johnson & Jago's yard at Leigh-on-Sea. She was built entirely of teak, even down to the locker sides and drawers, and as a result she was found to be too heavy for Maurice and Coppie, so she was sold.

They returned to *Lone Gull*, but Coppie was to find that the "kind sailing weather" she had enjoyed on the Blackwater was pretty infrequent.

"I had to face up to all weathers and was often scared. However, I was determined not to upset Maurice's sailing, so I persevered and he was very patient and kind.

"One perfect day with a beautiful calm sea I took myself to task and said, 'This fear must stop. You admire the sailing people you meet - they must get frightened at times and put it behind them, you must do the same.' So I smiled up at Maurice on the helm and just then he said, 'I think now is a good time for me to teach you what to do in case I fall overboard.'"

Amazingly, Coppie did persist. She fought her seasickness, overcame the lack of strength in her arms and became a capable helmswoman, taking a night watch aboard *Lone Gull* while Maurice and Fid Harnack slept below during their return from that promised, but postponed, trip to Holland.

Lone Gull, now moored in Besom Fleet at West Mersea, was a 37-mile drive from the Shenfield home.

"I got the idea it would be good to have a boat within walking distance of the house," says Maurice. Coppie had made a superb job of modernising a rather bland Edwardian house into a readily marketable home and, ever keen to improve another property, they moved to Chalkwell, near Westcliff-on-Sea, in 1949. Maurice bought the home of a former YM advertiser, Wilfred Watts, who ran his yacht charter business from Seaglimpse in the Leas Gardens.

Maurice soon changed the name to Swatchway because he could see the Jenkin Swatch buoy winking away across Sea Reach from his bedroom window.

He then bought *Wind Song*, the first boat he had ever designed, as her shoal draught would be ideal for the mud and pebble flats off Chalkwell railway station. Maurice stepped aboard his train to Fenchurch Street each morning and before dipping into his 'Daily Telegraph' looked longingly out towards his boat.

She was looked after by longshoreman Fred Ayres. However, having a half tide mooring on a hard foreshore did not suit Maurice and after two years at Chalkwell, a time in which Coppie got to work with DIY, they moved again - back to Shenfield.

One of the removal men dryly observed as he lifted a trunk he recognised, "The handle came off this one last time."

Norman Clackson told Coppie, "I bet you're making a

profit on every house, which is just as well as you are God's gift to estate agents and lawyers."

Maurice returned to Mersea for his mooring and this time with yet another of his own designs - *Tamaris*, a seven ton canoe stern bermudian yawl. She was 28.5ft long x 8.2ft x 4.5ft and influenced by Maurice's admiration for Albert Strange.

Yet though he sailed her for three years, Maurice was still restless. *Tamaris* was not as well balanced as he had hoped. He believed that with time and money a series of models could be built that would produce the perfect bermudian ketch, but instead he produced another book, 'Dream Ships', into which he poured all his knowledge, complete with many of his designs, in the hope that it would help somebody build his own ideal yacht.

"Having been born under the sign of Gemini, I was forever restless and inclined to seek something else," Maurice wrote.

There were to be a further two books published in the early 1950s, 'Everyman's Yachting' in 1952 and 'Sailing on a Small Income' the following year.

The latter was an update of his first ever book and harked back to the early attraction Maurice found with small boats - the cabin.

A chapter headed, 'Comfort on Board is the Thing', lists eight do's and dont's for happy order down below.

For the cabin sole we learn that lino is acceptable, "but remains damp underneath"; coconut matting and carpet are ruled out unless they can be stowed when the boat is underway; rubber perishes; hardwood floorboards are favourite.

Clothing kept in closed lockers will grow a fur of mildew, so "take the door off".

Tinned foods should be stowed away from sloshing bilges - otherwise labels wash off and the crew members never know what they're having for dinner.

Sugar and salt to be kept in screw top jars.

Boil spuds in seawater and save on fresh.

Milk can be kept fresh with the addition of formalin "from any chemist", but "use two drops only per pint, as in quantity it solidifies milk and is poisonous!"

"Don't let your wife (or anyone else's) cover the shelves of all lockers with 'nice clean paper'," Maurice advises, as paper gets damp.

Finally, "wash" greasy plates with "screws" of newspaper.

Such folksy advice was out of kilter with his next choice of boat, *Donna T*. A seven ton, 35-footer, she was an enlarged Dragon with the characteristic pencil-fine ends. She would be the last boat Maurice owned that was not of his own design.

23

East Coast Rivers

In the spring of 1954 Maurice returned to another of his old haunts, the little lock flanked on one side by a pebble path and ancient pub and on the other by the harbourmaster's house. The dribbling lock gates muzzled the seaward end of the Chelmer Canal. Heybridge Basin hadn't changed much since those salad days of the 1930s.

It was while Maurice was fitting out *Donna T* in the calm, fresh water of the canal that he first met Jack Coote.

Jack had bought a clumsy old centreboarder, *Iwunda*, from Priors at Burnham a couple of years before. His only experience of sailing, apart from a holiday on the Broads, had been on Regents Park Lake in London. While hospitalised suffering from a bout of jaundice, he had seen *Iwunda* advertised in 'Yachting Monthly' and was in a panic to buy her as "I thought everybody would be after her".

Jack made a swift recovery and became the proud owner of the 34-footer constructed by a "furniture builder" at Leigh-on-Sea. She had bunk cushions upholstered in red velvet and leaked like a sieve. Once, upon running ashore at Paglesham, there was so much water in her bilge it ran forward and jerked his crew overboard!

After a few copper tingles had been tacked on by Frank Shuttlewood, however, Jack sailed away to discover the Blackwater, a river that bewitched him so that he wrote a piece "In Praise of the Blackwater", which he submitted to a man who understood leaky old hookers and with whom, through his books, he already empathised - Maurice Griffiths.

Maurice was immediately struck by the detailed sketches of the creeks Jack had investigated and the soundings he had taken. Maurice thought Jack's exhaustive measurements too long and technical for a one off piece, but had, rather, a series of articles in mind, which would take in other estuary rivers as well.

He wrote back to Jack and said:

"You will probably know, and have no doubt used, John Irving's 'Rivers and Creeks of the Thames Estuary' which we originally published nearly 30 years ago and which was re-issued by Captain O M Watts before the war. This was an excellent volume of its kind, but some of the charts were not very legible and many of the directions as well as the soundings have become obsolete. We think that there is a need for a renewal of these sketch charts for the upper reaches and creeks and yachtsmen's anchorages in the Thames Estuary, and if you could compile some of this for us we should like to discuss the matter with you by arrangement ..."

In this way 'East Coast Rivers' was born. One of the most popular of all British pilot books, the first edition, published in 1956, carried a photograph of *Iwunda* surrounded by the sedge grass of Horsey Mere in the Walton Backwaters, with Jack's near naked daughters Janet and Judy, then aged seven and three respectively, kicking their heels over the coamings in the summer sunshine. It was a photograph that was quintessentially East Coast yachting, having more to do with land than sea.

Still in publication today, it has, since its first edition, been compiled with the help of East Coast yachtsmen who have sent in details of the latest soundings, where the nearest water tap is and so on; an act of rare civic charity.

In the first edition, boats as different as *Betty II*, a 6 ton centreboard cutter from Leigh, where she is still in commission incidentally, and *Alan*, a 15 ton auxiliary ketch based at Orford, and their owners are listed in the acknowledgements.

While Maurice held great appeal for impoverished yachtsmen with their bargain-basement boats, he was also taken seriously by the top end of the market and so he came to design a 40ft ketch with a wishbone rig for General Sir Frederick Browning, husband of novelist Daphne du Maurier. While the boat, *Jeanne d'Arc*, was under construction at the Fowey yard owned by Browning, both Maurice and Coppie went down on several social visits to the Brownings' home.

Coppie recalls, "I was thrilled when the invitation came to go and stay at Menabilly with Daphne and Tommy (as Daphne du Maurier called her husband). Daphne proved to be so charming - coming out of her dream world to converse with this ordinary housewife.

"Menabilly was a cold, draughty mansion - no heating apart from fires and small, round paraffin heaters. Parts of

Jeanne d'Arc

the building were in ruins and on one March visit we heard a few great crashes as more collapsed."

Jeanne d'Arc, with a 6ft 6in draught and canoe stern, was very much becoming a departure from Maurice's work. The shoal draught design was coming now to dominate his output as never before.

"The English yachtsman has been terribly, terribly conservative," he said. "It has been only since the 1950s that shallow-draught boats have been taken seriously. And they came about simply because people couldn't get deepwater moorings, they were all full up, and had to keep their boats on half tide moorings."

Donna T lasted just a year and then Maurice designed and built *Sequence*, a 34ft, 10 ton bermudian sloop. For two years he enjoyed the old sailing grounds of the East Coast before the demands of the drawing board obliged him to sell the boat in 1956 and for five years Maurice was high and dry.

"At this time we had started running build-it-yourself designs and every weekend I seemed to be doing wretched drawings, so there seemed hardly any point in having a boat," says Maurice.

In that time he produced the Eventide 24, which complied with the criteria of DIY building, was seaworthy

Sequence

enough for a family of four in estuary waters and yet light enough to be road trailered home for winter.

Humble though the design might have appeared, it impressed one Lieutenant Commander Edward Atkinson, based in Singapore, sufficiently to build one of them in 1958 and sail her home to Emsworth the following year.

With an 8ft beam she had a draught of 2ft 2in and sat upright on the mud with her twin bilge keels. Atkinson's boat was named after the insect that had an appetite for the plywood they built her of - *Borer Bee*. During her 8,000 mile voyage she proved to be a stiff sailer and a strong hulled yacht. She survived being swept onto coral in the Red Sea, where a swell dropped her bodily several times onto the reef.

More than 500 were built before YM readers started to demand a larger version. Soon Maurice had produced the Eventide 26. More than 1200 of both lengths have been built.

Still there was demand for an even shallower cruiser. Maurice thought back to his days aboard the barge-yacht *Curlew* and next produced the Waterwitch. Again there were two versions - the barge type with a 2ft draught and the Mark 1 version with bilge keels and a 3ft draught.

Maurice himself admitted the barge version was often derisively described as a 'sailing caravan', but he cared not, for that is exactly what was being requested. Nevertheless some of these floating caravans made impressive voyages.

MG locates an Eventide in a lost creek

(Opposite top) Lone Gull II in Spithead. MG and Coppie on board

(Below) MG's drawing of a well designed cabin

One, *Iota* complete with her leeboards was shipped from Australia to the Pacific Islands, which she then explored. The same method was used by the owner of the boat to sail throughout the West Indies. Maurice was proud that his creek crawlers were proving to be ocean rovers as well. At least two of the bilge keel versions completed round the world voyages.

One of his disappointments was the Cordelia design. He did not agree with the client's insistence on a pointed 'Scottish' stern. He felt it made the boat's aft lines too pinched and made the cockpit cramped and uncomfortable, while losing sailing buoyancy.

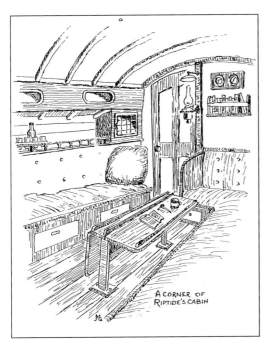

A CORNER OF RIPTIDE'S CABIN

"After four or five of these boats were built I discarded the plans as I really didn't want any more to my name," he says.

The next revolutionary material Maurice was to utilise was glassfibre.

"The GRP business in Britain started tentatively in the 1950s," Maurice remembers. "But as soon as people got used to it, firms that had nothing to do with boats - those that produced sanitary fittings and domestic items - started to build boats. GRP boatbuilding took off and never looked back.

"I always welcomed change.

I'm all for introducing new methods and better materials. I'm afraid I'm not much of a traditionalist. I love beautifully built yachts with splendid woods like teak and the best mahogany and so forth, but I also see the great advantages in the plastic yacht or the steel yacht, and of course if you can afford it, the aluminium yacht."

His next success was the Golden Hind 31, first as a single chine marine ply design and later as a double chine boat. With steel bilgekeel plates and an iron ballast keel, like the Eventides, over 250 of these yachts were to be built in a yard at Plymouth within the next two decades. Using very strong and simple construction with a transom stern, where the pintles and hangings of the outboard rudder were at once accessible for repair, these sturdy yachts appealed strongly to elderly

couples as a cruising retirement home. More than seventy, largely under American ownership, have made Atlantic crossings (to date a record for any single design class of yacht) and several have completed leisurely circumnavigations.

The growing population of Essex, combined with electrification of the rail line to London, meant overcrowded trains and Maurice often found himself standing all the way to Liverpool Street. Therefore another move was decided upon and after recommendation from a friend, the couple moved to a converted coach house in Haslemere, Surrey.

After his long break without a boat, Maurice designed himself another Lone Gull. *Lone Gull II* was 28ft long with a very

(Below)
MG aboard
Lone Gull II

MG's drawing
of a Waterwitch

generous 9ft beam and 3.2 foot draught with bilge keels. A
steady and seakindly boat, she was built at Harry Feltham's
yard in Portsmouth. Maurice now found himself a South
Coast man though his boat was very much an East Coast
type.

For the next few years, while they lived at Haslemere, he
and Coppie kept *Lone Gull II* at Hardway in Portsmouth
harbour. "It was before the South Coast had become packed
with yachts and power boats and we were able to explore at
weekends the harbours and creeks from Chichester to
Wareham and Poole," Maurice recalls.

"We came to love the ever changing colours of the Island
shore and the clear water of the Solent," he comments. It was
a love no doubt reinforced by *Lone Gull II*. With her
stabilising bilge keels, Coppie was never sick or scared on
board and as a result Maurice favoured the boat more than all
the others he had sailed, for now, at last, he had his wife
sailing regularly with him, a virtue that had eluded him with
Peter and that might have continued to elude him had Coppie
been obliged to sail in a more tender yacht.

"Coppie always preferred the Solent to the East Coast,"
Maurice says. "She found the scenery very pretty. 'The land
looks pleasanter,' she always said."

Of course, that land was more often horizontal too than at
some sickening angle, thanks to the stability of *Lone Gull II*.

24

Solent Sailing

Half way across the Channel, Maurice was using the head aboard *Lone Gull II* when he flinched as the National Anthem blared through the collapsible door. As a prank his crew had deliberately put the ship's radio beside the loo door just after the late night Shipping Forecast when BBC's Radio 4 plays the anthem.

"Well chaps it's a bit inconvenient," came Maurice's cool response.

His cruise to Cherbourg with Humberside yachtsmen Paul Haigh and Vincent Draper had been organised after Maurice had delivered a lecture to the Humber Yawl Club.

Paul Haigh, who for some years had owned a Lone Gull I class, *Mignonette*, had been there and persuaded Maurice to come and give a talk to the Grimsby & Cleethorpes Yacht Club while he was in the area. Paul put Maurice up and after the lecture Maurice said, "I wish I had a couple of chaps like you to sail with."

At this Vincent said, "You've got 'em. Where are we going?"

It was arranged that all three would cruise to France. Maurice received them at his Haslemere home where Paul remembers they were given smoked cod's roe sandwiches and tea before setting off.

"I noticed that his charts were ancient and his compass had a 10 degree easterly error, but never mind, we got there," said Paul later.

Maurice was very keen to take the night watch alone and the others turned in.

"He enjoyed it - the calm sea, in his own boat under stars alone, but with the knowledge that he had two gorillas down below if required."

Maurice remembers that night sail well. "For the whole of my watch I left the tiller adjusted with a ready-to-release tiller line and the steady old yacht held her course through the dark night waters."

Maurice Griffiths hoists the French courtesy flag while nearing Cherbourg on board Lone Gull II

Paul recalls that Maurice was a little queasy and deduced he was not used to the deep water swell.

At Cherbourg, Maurice remained aboard, releasing his crew to the delights of the port. When it was time to head back to the Solent, Paul went ashore to get some milk and was asked by Maurice to purchase some alcohol as well.

"I returned with a crate of wine," said Paul.

When *Lone Gull II* sailed home inside the Isle of Wight, Paul recalls being a little nervous on the helm.

"He quietly suggested I need not tack until the last minute; he said, 'Wait until you are close enough to blow your nose on his ensign as he passes.'"

Paul Haigh is just one of literally hundreds of yachtsmen Maurice has personally advised, written to and occasionally visited to discuss problems with their boats, but finally the requests became overwhelming.

"I had to employ a yacht designer, Kenneth Gibbs, to provide the answers, but he too got flooded out. Weeks went past and I didn't get any sailing in at all," Maurice comments. "It all got out of hand. Really it's much more profitable to design yachts for wealthy people."

There had been 140 designs from Maurice's drawing board and more than 2,000 boats launched.

He was being acknowledged in clubs throughout England for his services, having been elected for honorary life membership with the Royal Harwich YC, the Cruising Association, the Little Ship Club, the West Mersea YC and the Eventide Owners' Association.

For an unhappy year the Griffiths moved to Aldeburgh in Suffolk. They had been lured to the elegant little town by an old school friend of Maurice's who promised a mooring off the Aldeburgh Yacht Club. Maurice would be back on his home coast, the friend urged.

"Although it was a wrench for Coppie to leave our charming little Haslemere house and garden, the thought of another home that could be restored and improved was a challenge to her," said Maurice.

They soon moved into a detached house with views across the seaside town.

The Aldeburgh branch train with its connection to London would be too long a journey for daily commuting and so Maurice also rented a small flat near Baker Street. He found the short bus journey to work, after years of commuting, a huge relief. In the week Coppie explored the capital, which she hardly knew, while Maurice was at work, and at weekends they both returned to Aldeburgh.

It was while they were here that Maurice retired after 40 years at the helm of 'Yachting Monthly'.

"We retired to our windswept home," Maurice says. "And charming old town though Aldeburgh had once been with its fishermen's cottages and lifeboat station, living there was not quite what it had been cracked up to be. It seemed it was divided into separate cliques, which seldom spoke to one another. At the summit were those involved with the Benjamin Britten concerts and the Aldeburgh Festival, then the various bridge groups kept mainly to themselves, the artists displayed their shows in almost every third house in the High Street, the golf clique, calling themselves 'goafers' were a race apart, while at the yacht club feelings often ran high between the local racing classes. If one clique had a party you had to have a better one.

Lone Gull II *in Cherbourg*

"It was perhaps the frequent cold winds of the place that insinuated the sense of illusion. The miles of bleak shingle beach seemed to attract searching winds off the North Sea which created a local fashion - women regularly ventured out into the High Street with faces tightly wrapped in scarves, only their pinched noses recognisable."

One morning Maurice found Coppie in tears. The open hearted North Country lass could not bear the odd bohemian capriciousness of her neighbours and begged him to promise they would move.

To suit Coppie's love of the country and to escape the misery and mists of Aldeburgh a move inland was agreed. This time it would be Coppie's interests that would be served by the move.

They found a Tudor farmhouse near Stratford St Andrew

- 10 miles inland from Aldeburgh. The adjacent farm was being worked by Earl Cranbrook and Coppie, who had long enjoyed visits to a Northampton farm, welcomed the opportunity to be among farm animals again. The 15th century house with its Dutch gable end had been modernised inside, but still Coppie eagerly made mental lists of improvements she was to organize.

Surrounded by fields and woodlands and a water meadow, with the upper reaches of the River Alde running through it, it was all one could wish for, even when a high tide coincided with heavy rain and brought the river into the garden, flooding the cesspit.

It was 'real' country living and Maurice did his best to show enthusiasm for "constant repairs" to broken gates, tumbledown fences, boundary ditches, choked pipes, roof tiles, gutters and drains.

He smiled thinly at the inquisitive cows whose hooves turned their paddock into a bog.

Soon Maurice realised he would have no time for a long held ambition - to design and build a boat for his retirement.

In correspondence with a fellow yacht designer, Maurice admitted that "Having had eight houses since the end of the war Marjorie and I are fairly well acquainted with the uncertainties and disappointments inseparable from home-seeking. It's even worse than trying to find the ideal ship."

An Eventide off the Naze

To Maurice's relief Coppie surrendered - she had indulged her love of life in a farmhouse and admitted the workload was

*MG at
The Yachting
Monthly office,
1959*

now beyond them. They found another home, this time on the outskirts of Woodbridge with a view of the river... a distant view of the river!

In the mid-sixties Maurice was approached by one Phil Sheaf, an Eventide owner, complaining about excessive weather helm. In a long and detailed letter Maurice candidly admitted it was a problem, but one which most V-bottomed shallow draught hulls suffered. As Mr Sheaf was intending to enlarge his 24ft Eventide into the 26ft version, Maurice advised him on what measures to take to eradicate the weighty helm, namely moving the bilge keels and enlarging the rudder. Mr Sheaf was suitably impressed, so much so that he actually started selling MG designs some eight years later and since then has acted as Maurice Griffith's design agent.

He has had difficulty with Maurice's old drawings - they are mostly done with pencil on to tracing paper. Maurice is dismissive of state-of-the-art design, once commenting to Phil: "Hm, have computer will design."

Maurice explained it had taken him 18 months to learn how to programme his TV video, to which Phil added that he knew of children who could handle them while licking ice-cream at the same time.

"That just about sums it up. Look can you find out who these children are and send them along?" asked Maurice.

When it came to the beauty or otherwise of his more popular designs, Maurice was not in the habit of wearing rose-coloured spectacles. He once told his successor to the editorship of YM, Des Sleightholme, "If ever you see a barrel or a box with rudder and sails it'll be one of my designs."

It was in 1967 that Des arrived at the "garret office suite", as he described YM's Lincolns Inn premises, in preparation to take over from Maurice.

"I had regarded him with a certain awe, indeed I found him a bit daunting, a rather severe figure, correct, establishment, with a precise manner of speaking and a direct, level eye," Des recalls.

Indeed Maurice inspired silent respect from those in the office. Not least because in rare moments of temper loss he grabbed a book as a means of venting his frustration by hurling it across the office. The book would invariably be a Lloyd's Register!

The "garret" office had once been the HQ of the Suffragettes, a link that intrigued Maurice, and Des's first impression of it is like something Charles Dickens might have experienced: "A place of sloping roofs, bubbling gas fires and windows caulked with newspaper against the howling winter rains."

Then there were just seven staff running the magazine: Maurice, Associate Editor Kathy Palmer, General Manager Norman Clackson, Advertising Assistant George Turland, and three female secretaries.

After the bohemian and jovial atmosphere of the 'Yachts & Yachting' editorial offices, the YM office seemed a little cool to Des, who introduced himself thus: "Hello, everybody calls me Des."

"Really," said Kathy. "Well I suppose that's your misfortune."

Each one of the executives in turn warned Des of the others.

Des worked alongside Maurice for just a short month before Norman, Kathy and Maurice all retired within a week of each other.

"When I leave YM," Maurice told Des. "I will give you no advice, suggest nothing, make no comment, she's your ship now. If ever you want help though, you've only to ask."

Maurice left a successful magazine with a circulation of 40,000.

Des appreciated such a clean severance; indeed he acted in the same manner when he too retired. "It is the right way of it," he said.

Maurice had sold *Lone Gull II* back in 1963. Now he was without boat or magazine, but there were still more books and more

MG is entertained on a Dutch yacht at Tollesbury in 1984. Tony Purnell is second from right

designs to come. Two years before his retirement Coppie and Maurice had moved house yet again, this time to Woodbridge in Suffolk. While living there he had a few chance meetings with children's author, Arthur Ransome, who was in the last years of his life.

One thing both authors had in common was the trying experience of 'fans'. Ransome often bewailed the visits made to him by parents hoping their children would be inspired in some peculiar way.

"I always remember him saying," said Maurice. "'Oh these pestilential parents who bring these awful kids.'"

Before he retired, Maurice had made another friend in Woodbridge - Tony Purnell, one of the 'Around the coast' correspondents for 'Yachting Monthly'. He gave Tony a leg up in making contacts for his work by introducing him to numerous people at the Royal Harwich Yacht Club. He also advised him on writing.

"He told me you must always have deadlines," said Tony. "Even when you retire. He always gives himself deadlines - says they're good for you! He would come up and do a grand tour of yacht clubs and I would bask in the reflected glory."

Tony noticed how Maurice always wore correct dress at the clubs - tie and reefer jacket - but how on the water in smock or oilskin that you could not "tell him from anyone else".

"He would not suffer fools gladly. Once he saw someone dressed up like mad at Mersea and said, 'I bet they haven't been further than the Nass.'"

On his "grand tours", Maurice often returned to the Walton Backwaters, by road, with Tony. They would visit Landermere, Beaumont and Kirby.

"He wasn't sentimental about it or nostalgic. He just liked

it there. He would tell me how he used to sail up these creeks and surround himself with grass and reeds - that was the thing about him; he never talked of the gales and fogs all the time as so many yachting people do, but of the quiet times. If he did say things were a bit hard then you knew it was blowing a hoolie," said Tony.

Despite increasing longsightedness - "Eyesight can be something of a problem, and quite a limiting factor on the amount of work one can get through each day. I do find collecting notes, writing and rewriting text, and then typing the damn stuff very trying ...," - Maurice continued at his drawing board and typewriter. He was understandably vexed when evidence of design plagiarism was produced by Phil Sheaf.

"I am much obliged to you for letting me know about your customer, as this does appear a clear case of 'lifting' published plans for private use," Maurice wrote to Phil.

He wrote directly to the offender, diplomatically offering advice on construction, thereby providing an opportunity to remind him whose design it was. "The world is full of cribbers," he told Phil.

The plans produced by YM for home building enraged the established yacht designers as they were around £25 for a set of plans for a 26-footer - five times less than comparable 'professional' designs.

Phil had now embarked on a design correspondence course and Maurice candidly encouraged his efforts, "Rather like learning to write, the more actual drawing you do the more you learn, for practice is the principal thing towards acquiring a sense of proportion in the hull design, fairness of lines, awareness of how much space there is in various parts of the boat. I find it very difficult and time consuming."

Since the far off days of his yacht agency, Maurice had grown weary of time wasters, people who spent hours looking over boats without the slightest intention of buying one.

In a letter to Phil he complained of the breed increasing. "At the Southampton Boat Show there were more visitors just looking, more exhibits, but not perhaps so much money changing hands. I have the feeling that there are a damn sight too many boat shows in the country: too many firms wanting to jump on to the bandwagon. I think the Brighton and Ipswich shows showed this in disappointing business results. In any case I cannot fathom the thinking that decided on a highly expensive yacht base at Brighton with no good shelter on either side of it for many miles."

25

Disabled At Sea

I n 1971 Maurice designed the yacht for his retirement. *Kylix* was a seven ton, centreboard bermudian cutter, 27ft long and, with the plate raised, had a draught of just 3ft. After a break of almost nine years, Maurice was afloat in his own craft once more, but *Kylix* was to be his last and her doghouse represented Maurice's first passion; it was shaped like the cab of a railway engine.

Frank Knights, the Woodbridge yacht builder and last Trinity House pilot for the Deben, was approached by Maurice to lay him a mooring.

"Maurice ferreted out his own spot for it in the lower part of Troublesome Reach," said Frank.

"I think Maurice knew the river, between the wars anyway, better than I did. I certainly never piloted him in. That can be a nasty old place, the entrance; we lost a couple of fishermen a couple of years back. They was cutting through one of the swatches and that was blowing hard. A sea came and broke aboard, flooded the cockpit and broke 'em up."

Maurice held great respect for the Deben bar ever since his drama with *Dabchick* there in the 1920s, but in *Nightfall* too, he had had a hair-raising experience back in 1932. With her draught of 3ft 3in and the pressure of a train to catch back to London and just half an hour of ebb left to run, Maurice decided there would be 4ft of water in the entrance.

"With the sea like a mirror in the haze, and with only a slight swell coming in to cause the shingle banks

Kylix. *27ft CB bermudian cutter designed by MG, built by F Smeeth, Dedham, Essex in 1971. The last yacht owned by MG, and sold in 1976*

on each side of the bar to murmur like a burst of clapping on the radio (how different from the angry roar of this place when there was a fresh onshore breeze blowing!) I steered *Nightfall* up to the little black barrel buoy and looked for the two leading marks amongst the houses at the Ferry.

"Sitting relaxed with my right arm over the tiller I saw that we were only just creeping up against the tide: it was still flowing out faster than I had expected, and although I opened the throttle wide, the engine, gamely thumping its oversize propeller round, was making painfully slow progress over the ground. I had perhaps forgotten how any boat under power draws her stern down, and further, how this effect can be aggravated while she is in shallow water and the keel 'smells the bottom'. I should have considered that in these very conditions *Nightfall,* as she struggled along, was probably drawing as much as 4ft."

Maurice Griffiths aboard his Kylix, *1976 (the last year he owned her)*

Maurice tried to edge *Nightfall* in out of the worst of the tide and her head, caught by the current, fell off and she hit the shingle.

"Immediately the tiller slammed over against the coaming with the press of water against the rudder, and I found myself helplessly pinned in the corner of the cockpit. In an agonising movement poor old *Nightfall* lurched over until her lee deck was under and the water poured round her bow and stern and lapped close to the top of the cockpit coaming. My God, MG, I couldn't help thinking, you've done all the wrong things and you've bloody well asked for it. There've been scores of vessels of all kinds lost on this bar, so you can't claim to be the first by a long chalk!"

The flood tide rescued him and years later when creating *Kylix*, Maurice had the Deben bar in mind when he shaved another 3in off her keel!

In *Kylix* Maurice returned to the creeks he first explored in *Swan*. At first the Walton Backwaters did not appear any different: "... this area of meres and mud-flats, of rotting posts and withies waving in the tide, of creeks that meandered

mysteriously behind sedge covered islets, and of the pungent smell of seaweed mingled with the cries of waders feeding along the tideline ..."

MG aboard Kylix

But then "a faintly persistent murmur of an outboard engine became louder as a bright red speedboat appeared round the point and headed down the creek."

The curse of the waterskier left the yachts "jigging and dancing" in their wash and Maurice's crew, a wildfowler, wishing that he was armed with his 12-bore.

"Nobody, we assured ourselves, wanted to stop other people from enjoying their chosen sport," Maurice wrote. "But this display of callous ignorance was too much to bear in silence."

In general though he still obtained great satisfaction from his old haunts. A simple week's cruise he logged thus to Phil Sheaf: "From Levington we sailed to the mouth of the Colne for the first night (wind light E), next day to the Burnham river and a night in Brandy Hole. Up to Hullbridge, then down to an anchorage for the night in the Roach; next day Paglesham and on to the Colne and a night in Pyefleet Creek. A visit to Wivenhoe, then with a fresh N breeze a fine sail and beat up towards Harwich and into Hamford Water; next day into Harwich and up to Wrabness in the Stour, and the last day a fine beat up the Orwell to Ipswich against a fresh NW breeze, and back to Levington: 150 miles in all, and 14 hours under engine.

"I hope your business permits you to get away at times for some sailing. It is a great tonic."

In the autumn of 1974 *Kylix* was hit by a hail squall while under way in the Deben. Maurice put his crew on the helm and made his way forward to take in sail.

"The deck started getting white with hail and I hurried forward to pull the staysail down. The next thing I can remember was shooting forward and my left foot must have got caught under the windlass. I turned over and there was a very loud crack and it was quite painful," Maurice recounted.

He had jammed his leg under the windlass, then pitched over the top of it cracking his kneebone and spraining his leg. Almost helpless, Maurice was grateful he had his muscular pal Dick Ryland, an ex-Merchant seaman, as crew that day.

After three weeks in Anglesea Road Hospital, Ipswich, Maurice was left pondering his fate - what would he have done had he been singlehanded? He was still sailing regularly on his own.

"Marjorie said, 'Well you'd better not sail alone again if you can go back to the boat at all.' And there was nothing for it. I had to sell the boat, which was a great pity. I was then 74," he said.

The following year Maurice went deepwater cruising in luxury with Coppie, aboard the *Pendennis Castle*, for a six-week round trip to South Africa.

Though he was now boatless once more, there were plenty of offers of berths. Phil Sheaf actually put his boat *Sigurd Syr* at Maurice's disposal. "I am touched by your generosity," Maurice told him. "For I always rate the loan of a man's boat as equivalent to - or at least nearly so - the loan of his wife!"

During his last busy years at YM, Maurice had time to produce just one book - the 'Arrow Book of Sailing', published in 1966, but since his retirement he has written three, all published in the 1970s - 'Swatchways and Little Ships', 'Man the Shipbuilder' and 'The First of the Tide'.

In the last years of 1970 Maurice started researching for a book he had been asked to write about mine warfare. He returned to HMS *Vernon* where, after 34 years, he said he felt like Father Neptune. While en route across the country to and from Portsmouth during the winter of 1979, he was angered by what he described as "the striking class".

Recalling his own impecunious days he told Phil Sheaf: "... I have fair recollections of what it is like to be almost penniless and dependent on any sort of job that one could get and the position of the underdog has been experienced. But the behaviour and attitude of so many (not all, thank goodness) working people - the striking class - in view of all the benefits they enjoy now makes me somewhat bitter at times."

Even during his days as Editor of YM, Maurice, on reflection, felt he and his contemporaries had pitifully short holidays compared with the modern equivalent. When Phil told Maurice of his own holiday, a visit to Disneyland in California, he replied, "I would not have cared for the Walt Disneyland part. That made us both shudder!"

It was during this period of his life that Maurice was approached by the traditional sail author, Robert Simper. He wanted to interview Maurice for his book 'Gaff Sail'.

Maurice told him: "I have spent years trying to get rid of the gaff rig in my designs and now you have gone and brought it back!"

Robert believed Maurice was "brilliant" at promoting his designs and ideas, but myths grew up round him in the process.

"It was widely believed in Old Gaffers Association circles that Maurice Griffiths was a great supporter of the gaff rig and old boats generally. In fact he hated the gaff rig and told me he had designed very few gaff boats since the 1930s."

Though not a traditionalist, Maurice simply is anti-gaff on boats over 25ft long. One of his own designs, a Tidewater 30,

A smack yacht in a breeze
Maurice Griffiths

was built as a gaff cutter for her owner who had a family, but after a few seasons was converted to bermudian at considerable cost, as he found the gear too heavy. Nevertheless Maurice said he was well aware of the advantages of the gaff rig, such as the ability to trice up the tack so as to be able to see the buoy when coming on to a mooring and also the capacity with gaff for scandalising the main. Again when coming on to a mooring it enables the skipper to take a third of the mainsail off her yet still have steerage way.

The reason Maurice is associated with traditional sail is simply that his best books have been written about boats now thought of as traditional. When Maurice was sailing in them and writing about them, however, they were contemporary. The writing, unlike the vehicles, is timeless.

Paul Gelder, currently Features Editor of 'Yachting Monthly', also experienced the collapse of a myth. During an interview with Maurice he was told:

"When you look back at the trouble we had with old wooden boats, leaky topsides, decks and skylights, I can't abide people who are prejudiced. We were often asked at Boat Shows: 'Why do you advertise these dreadful bathtubs?' If I could have a boat now I wouldn't mind a GRP one."

Paul wrote: "There was a heart-stopping pause before he added, thoughtfully, 'Though I think a well-built wooden one takes a lot of beating.'"

Were Maurice to return to sailing in the 1990s he would also opt for a bilgekeeler: "I wish I'd had one at Chalkwell."

Not all yachts being launched today get Maurice's blessing, however. The Fastnet disaster in 1979 when 15 yachtsmen were lost brought this criticism from him.

"It showed under these extreme conditions how very unseaworthy these modern conception racing yachts can be. Very broad, very shallow, very light boats. They turned over quite easily; not only that but having turned over they continued floating upside down because of their great beam and light keel. It also showed how very unprepared some of those boats were for bad weather. It was an exceptional gale, but the Fastnet has been sailed more than once in nasty gales.

"What I object to very much is that the manufacturers are selling racing boats with deep keels and spade rudders as family cruisers, and they aren't suitable for that at all."

As for satellite navigation, Maurice once commented to Tony Purnell: "Do you know what, very soon we'll be able to sit in our houses and say: 'Yacht go to Calais'. And it'll go on its own."

Before moving to Mersea Island the Griffiths had eight years at Woodbridge, a period in which Maurice branched out into larger designs. At the Conyer Marine yard in Kent, the Spears family were producing a number of yachts in steel, which they called the Bay Class.

The firm's consultant naval architect at the time was Robert Hundy, who had previously served for 17 years with a shipyard in Holland building steel barges and yachts.

Eager to increase his knowledge of the techniques for small craft of steel construction, holding that "An old dog is never too far gone to learn new tricks", Maurice was glad to collaborate with the Spears-Hundy combine. For the next few years he and Bob Hundy in collaboration designed a number of handsome steel cruising yachts, which ranged from 39ft to 58ft on deck.

"The more I learnt about steel construction," said Maurice. "The more I realised its superiority as a material for yachts over a certain size in its great strength and its watertightness over other materials except perhaps light alloy. I managed to imbibe a lot from the patient Bob's experience."

Some years later Maurice heard how one of his own steel yachts of the 31ft 6in Hacathian class (a single chine ketch with bilge keel plates similar to the Waterwitch) was on a four month northern cruise. She had sailed round Kap Farvel, the most southerly point of Greenland, to escape from a hard nor'wester and seek shelter off the southeast coast in Denmark Strait. Here she became trapped in the pack ice and held fast. The stern davits were crumpled and the yacht was in great danger of being crushed. It was only her strength that enabled the boat to work herself clear of the grinding masses with her diesel engine and escape into clear water.

26

The Last Cruise

Surrounded by the shoals of the Thames Estuary, Maurice found security on Mersea Island, which is cut off by the tide when the ancient Roman causeway floods on springs. His retirement was settled by the constancy of the ebb and flow through the mud gullies in the saltings.

At the other end of the country Peter Gerard was now alone with the deep water of St Mawes in Cornwall for comfort. Chas Pears had died back in the 1950s. *Shenandoah* was played at his funeral. Peter was very lonely and her sister, who had won a car in a raffle, gave it to the pining widow.

Peter took 13 tests before she eventually obtained her driving licence. After several disappointments she told the examiner she would put the car through a plate glass window if he didn't pass her the next time, but she failed again.

Norman Clackson, while on holiday in the Cornish village, coincidentally saw Peter during the 1970s.

"I was told to keep out of her way. I was amazed to see her. She had a little car there and everyone would jump to one side when they saw her coming. I was very surprised to see her. She didn't look much different from the distance I saw her."

Wanderer had long since been broken up after falling apart.

When *Juanita* fell off her own legs and stove in her bilge Peter never recovered, according to local shipwright Jimmy Green.

"The boat was sold for a few pounds and I personally feel this hastened Mrs Pears' end," he said. "She was a very difficult person to deal with, never happy unless causing friction amongst the workmen and fishermen. I spent a lot of time pouring oil over troubled waters.

"But after *Juanita* was sold she got dirty and scruffy. She didn't care any more. She lived like a tramp over some old boatsheds. She started going down hill and wandered about crying all the time."

Peter died in March 1980 aged 79.

Maurice meanwhile kept on writing.

In 1981 his book on the history of mine warfare, 'The Hidden Menace', was published with a bizarre prologue - the reader struggles to imagine a Third World War in which nuclear mines have been placed in the North Sea. Maurice hated writing this fiction, but his publishers thought it would be a marketable peg on which to hang such a study.

Yet it was not solely based on imagination - speculation of such a scenario had often been discussed at HMS *Vernon*. Again there were echoes of Erskine Childers.

Maurice's popularity was as strong as ever among readers of YM. He was asked every year to join the YM stand at the Earl's Court Boat Show to answer questions and meet the readers.

Des Sleightholme said, "He loved it and so did his old faithfuls who brought stacks of dog-eared books for him to autograph and quizzed him about his various boat designs."

On one day at the Boat Show he signed no less than 190 copies of 'The Hidden Menace'. One fan from the Humber bought six copies for fellow members of his yacht club.

Maurice still went to great lengths to help readers with their design bugbears. Here, for example, is his reply to a yachtsman suffering from lack of rudder control.

"I have given this phenomenon a good deal of thought, and have come to the conclusion that it all depends on the type of stream that is led to the rudder. For instance, if the yacht (or any kind of wooden vessel) has a thick sternpost which drags a column of dead water behind it, a streamlined rudder with fine trailing edge would have little effect. Only a flat sided rudder nearly as thick as the sternpost, and with a fairly square after edge, would act well in such disturbed water conditions.

"This, I think, accounted for the square ended rudders to be found on all old ships, with their enormous sternposts, and even amongst the faster and later (mid-19th century) sailing ships and clippers. In a yacht even a large fixed propeller could cause so much turbulence and dead water combined that a slim rudder with fine edge would have reduced effect. On the other hand, where there is a very fine and undisturbed run (as in a 12-Metre or any modern racing yacht) the narrow and deep rudder blade, streamed and fine-edged proves highly efficient. It all depends, therefore, on what the back end of the yacht is like: which must be the scientific statement of the month!"

Mr and Mrs Griffiths were now beginning to suffer the rigours of a long life. Coppie's legs were weakening, though a hip operation helped, and Maurice had emphysema, which he described variously as "like a tired rubber balloon or another form of osmosis" or "much panting like a Westinghouse brake pump", which left the pair "tottering from day to day propping each other up". These exacerbated by Maurice's abdominal pains, which he had suffered since his impoverished days in London, were making existence miserable at times.

He wrote to Phil Sheaf: "Believe me, Phil, it's hateful growing so old and tired when everyone thinks you look so bright and energetic, dammit!"

Old trooper that he was, Maurice turned out another two books in the 1980s - 'Round the Cabin Table' and 'Sixty Years a Yacht Designer' - his final tome. The year before he had been awarded the Royal Cruising Club medallion for services to yacht cruising.

His last sail at the grand old age of 83 was in 1980 with Des Sleightholme. They had made one or two modest cruises together and once, with another rather garrulous friend of Des's. On that occasion Des recalls: "After that trip MG rolled his eyes at me and said, 'I thought that bloody man would never draw breath, I almost wish I didn't like him.'"

During another cruise, just the two of them aboard, Maurice was at the helm when he ran Des's boat hard aground in the Deben.

"The tide was flooding and it was merely a case for putting the kettle on, but he was mortified lest anybody had seen *him* at the helm in a river that he once knew so well. Another boat went by. Maurice ducked below out of sight. He was well aware of the esteem in which he was held, of the image he must not tarnish," said Des.

Maurice was still great company down below. His anecdotes were, according to Des, "often highly scurrilous and concerning the sex lives of notable yachting personalities. MG has a wicked, irreverent and highly developed sense of humour. I remember as we sailed past Ramsholt Cliffs, which is marked on the chart as an anchorage, but which on that day was fully exposed and very uncomfortable, a small yacht lay at anchor there rolling her guts out. The owner spotted MG and started waving, grinning and squirming with pleasure."

Maurice waved back and between fixed and grinning lips muttered: "Yes you stupid prat the chart says anchor so down it goes."

On that very last sail they were anchored in Kirby Creek in Maurice's favourite Backwaters. Surrounded by peace and calm the pair sat in the cockpit with their gins and tonic listening to the redshanks, Des with his pipe, Maurice with a small cigar.

"Then came a runabout with some multicoloured berk on skis in its wake. They described various idiot gyrations, circled us, and sped off," said Des.

Maurice turned to him and said, "I don't really want to know any more. I keep seeing it as it *was*, as it was and can never be again, it's something different now, the creeks as I knew them are now not the creeks I wrote about."

Later Maurice told me: "We started from Woolverstone where he (Des) kept the boat and everywhere was so crowded with boats moving in all directions. And I thought I'll just have to accept it, I must give it up and so I did."

MG and Coppie at Coast Road, West Mersea

The days when Maurice could peg his helm and "get on with a bit of carpentry or something" were over - now he would have to be busy "watching out for the other chap".

On reflection Maurice added, "Yet even though I have very little contact now with that other world, the world of my past, I don't regret any of it. I never had any doubts about what I was doing in the sense that perhaps designing boats and writing about boats might be seen as a not particularly serious endeavour. I can't even say that I ever thought much about it. I was designing boats, editing a magazine, and writing books. It seemed perfectly all right to me."

Instead of participating in the sport he had spent a lifetime promoting, Maurice was content to watch, from his Mersea home, King's Hard, a split level dwelling on the Coast Road, the yachts batting about on the Blackwater, though sometimes even spectating he found harrowing.

"Except for the past few days this has been a very dreary summer, and sad for all you enthusiastic boat owners. Sitting in my chair in our little sunroom with the binoculars my heart has sometimes bled for the stalwarts braving the wind and rain in their orange waterproofs. Sometimes the sight is too much for me and, with my sensitive nature, I am driven to take refuge on the lower deck in my study where I can get on with my work without being able to look up and see them in their misery!" Maurice wrote of the summer of 1980.

That year Maurice and Coppie escaped the vagaries of British weather and took a sea cruise aboard *Canberra* to South America, returning via Madeira.

Eventually Maurice turned his back completely on the sea and moved away from the coast and up into the hinterland of Mersea where he designed his own "little igloo" as he called it - a bungalow where Coppie need no longer worry about negotiating stairs.

MG's last drawing for the author's yacht Powder Monkey

Although his eyes are not strong enough for the fine lines of design any more, Maurice very kindly made his last drawing for an improvement to the leaky forehatch of my own yacht *Powder Monkey*. She's a 30ft Yeoman Junior sloop designed by Alan Buchanan, a celebrated designer with whom Maurice collaborated while still Editor of 'Yachting Monthly'.

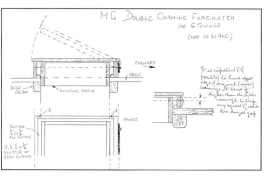

27

The Birthday Party

Maurice still ventures down to the waterside - he loves to lunch at the West Mersea Yacht Club where he is received with respect but without ceremony. It was this club that hosted his 90th birthday party. The two-day celebration was to include a barbecue on Packing Marsh Island, and a bar buffet with MG at the clubhouse on the Sunday, followed by a sail past.

It came at a time when I was boatless - having sold my centreboard cutter, *Almita*, some months beforehand. But it seemed only fitting to attend the bash by sea and so I hijacked a friend's boat and left Bradwell aboard *Sea Boots* with Tim Cornall on the Saturday. We had a sweltering day on the River Blackwater, sailing up for beer at Heybridge Basin, where I swam across to Doug Scurry's Maldon smack *Joseph T.*

After our spinnaker run up river we turned back down towards Mersea against a clammy light easterly. Even to windward it was so warm that Tim and I were dressed in bathers. Off St Lawrence Bay the weather turned from this choking hot summer breeze to a violent flash thunderstorm. In all my years sailing on this river, never have I seen conditions change so quickly.

The glittering isometric triangles of sunshine on brown-green wavelets became black 3ft high waves with their heads torn off into white spray, which hit us like horizontal hail.

In minutes we had on full oilskins, were double reefed and running back up river, it having been impossible to get further to windward.

The sky was black, low and fissured with orange bolts of lightning. To weather, the placid Blackwater actually looked frightening.

The cherubs on Maurice's life-chart were marking the old sailor's birthday too, it seemed.

As the storm abated, we put about and beat back up into Mersea Quarters. Some MG fans were blowing down

John Williams'
Eventide

through Mersea Fleet in an inflatable dinghy, their outboard engine failing to start. As we passed we threw them a line, which fell short, but they wallowed harmlessly up on the mud.

We passed John Williams (of the Eventide Owners' Association) in his own Eventide - painted in the Mersea oyster boat colours of park bench green and cream. In the cockpit under a dripping awning half a dozen or so children peered out into the black rainswept creek.

The barbecue on Packing Marsh Island was cancelled.

It mattered not, however, for these were true MG disciples and the inclement weather was good for their souls. It was what had happened to the man himself. They'd read it after all in his books. Marinas were for well-heeled cissies.

We did not venture ashore either that cold, wet night, but instead lay to a spare mooring in Thorn Fleet listening to the strains of Beatles songs coming from the yacht club, rising and falling through the dying wind and blowing away into the silence of Old Hall Marshes.

The next morning broke fine and clear. The storm had been short foretold, and therefore soon past as the old weather lore has it.

MG fans were already in evidence on their way to meet their boats' maker - inflatables towing inflatables to save on outboard petrol!

The dinghies were tethered on the West Mersea jetty as the oilskin clad brigade walked ashore beneath the council sign, which read: "Access to boats. Dangerous area. No skateboards, bicycles or motorcyles." Before the buffet those visitors who ventured into the bar smiled diffidently at the deliberately provocative offhand and high camp manner of the willowy, moustachioed, blonde, barman.

They felt more comfortable upstairs when a blazered Maurice arrived with Coppie and mingled with 80 or so guests over claret and hock.

Maurice was given many presents and Anglia TV was there filming for a new sailing series. 'Yachting Monthly' was, of course, there too, represented by Deputy Editor James Jermain.

After all those years Maurice still rankled about his first marriage and in his speech thanked his current wife, Coppie, for her promise of "atonement" to the virtues of wedlock, making his second choice one of love and happiness.

Later he sat on the foldaway chair provided for him down on the Coast Road and, through binoculars, rolled the yachts of the sail past - his yachts - into focus with an exclamation of delight as each one sailed by.

Appendix

From the Board of MG

A drawing of a typical barge yacht by Maurice, from the pages of Yachting Monthly

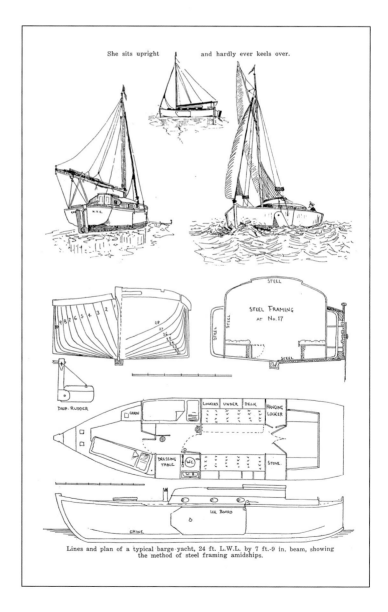

Lines and plan of a typical barge yacht, 24 ft. L.W.L. by 7 ft.-9 in. beam, showing the method of steel framing amidships.

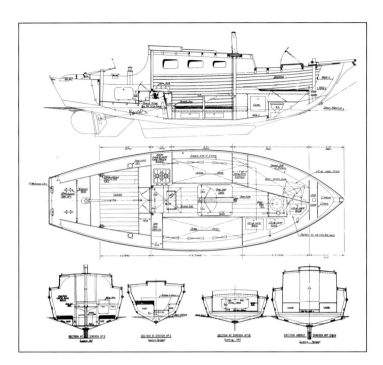

General layout plan of the 24ft version of the Eventide

MG's centre cockpit version of the Waterwitch design

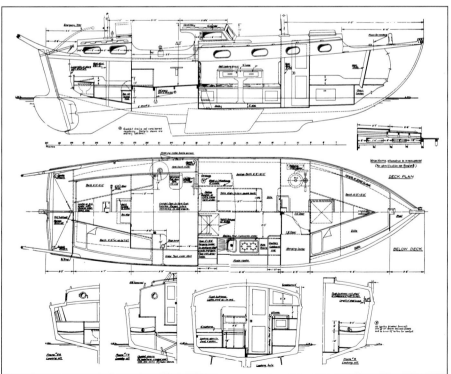